Addressing Forced Displacement through Development Planning and Co-operation

GUIDANCE FOR DONOR POLICY MAKERS AND PRACTITIONERS

This work is published under the responsibility of the Secretary-General of the OECD. The opinions expressed and arguments employed herein do not necessarily reflect the official views of OECD member countries.

This document, as well as any data and any map included herein, are without prejudice to the status of or sovereignty over any territory, to the delimitation of international frontiers and boundaries and to the name of any territory, city or area.

Please cite this publication as:
OECD (2017), *Addressing Forced Displacement through Development Planning and Co-operation: Guidance for Donor Policy Makers and Practitioners*, OECD Development Policy Tools, OECD Publishing, Paris. *http://dx.doi.org/10.1787/9789264285590-en*

ISBN 978-92-64-28558-3 (print)
ISBN 978-92-64-28559-0 (PDF)

Series: OECD Development Policy Tools
ISSN 2518-6248 (print)
ISSN 2518-3702 (online)

Nigeria. Victims of years of violent insurgency
Women in Kuya camp in northeast Nigeria in 2016 were generally the sole breadwinners for their families after most of their husbands were killed or abducted by Boko Haram militants during a years-long brutal insurgency.

Photo credits: Cover © UNHCR/Hélène Caux

Foreword

This guidance has been designed for development donors working in situations of forced displacement. It seeks to provide a clear and practical introduction to the challenges faced when working in situations of forced displacement, as well as some practical recommendations for donor staff seeking to mainstream responses to forced displacement into their development planning and co-operation.

It draws on findings from an extensive literature review and on exchanges with key stakeholders, including donors, host governments, United Nations agencies, international and national non-governmental organisations, civil society organisations, international financial institutions and the private sector. It also incorporates examples of lessons learned and good practices shared by Development Assistance Committee (DAC) member countries and observers.

In addition, the DAC Network on Development Evaluation (Evalnet) has contributed to this effort by producing a working paper, *Responding to Refugee Crises in Developing Countries: What Can We Learn From Evaluations*, that looks at lessons learned and key messages from Organisation for Economic Co-operation and Development (OECD) DAC members' evaluations related to forced displacement and in refugee contexts.

For the purposes of this guidance, forced displacement refers to the situation of persons forced to leave or flee their homes due to conflict, violence or human rights violations. The guidance does not address persons displaced by natural disasters or development projects; nor does it address regular or irregular migrants. While recognising the reality of mixed migration flows, the guidance focuses on refugees, internally displaced persons (IDPs) and returnees.

The distinction between refugees and regular or irregular migrants is retained because the legal frameworks addressing the needs of these two categories are vastly different, a fact which is of particular importance when considering solutions. Nevertheless, while international law draws a clear line between refugees and migrants in theory, readers are reminded that this distinction is often much more nuanced in practice, with groups and movements of migrants, refugees, and IDPs often overlapping at different points in time.

The guidance comprises three parts:

Part One outlines **the context** and introduces forced displacement and development issues. It includes background information on displacement trends and a summary of challenges in mainstreaming forced displacement into development planning.

Part Two sets out the **three broad priority areas of work**, where donors can significantly contribute to existing capacities at the national, regional and global levels with some examples of good practice and lessons learnt to provide practical illustrations for the reader.

Part Three highlights **twelve actions grouped into four key principles** outlining what donors need to do in order to be able to engage and programme more effectively and efficiently in situations of forced displacement.

Acknowledgements

The lead author of this publication is Annabel Mwangi, Policy Advisor at the Development Co-operation Directorate (DCD). Contributing authors were Laura Gamez and Lisanne Raderschall, Policy Analysts at the Development Co-operation Directorate. The development of the guidance was supervised by Brenda Killen, Deputy Director of the Development Co-operation Directorate.

The authors would like to thank the Co-Chairs of the DAC Temporary Working Group (TWG) on Refugees and Migration, Takuma Kajita (Japan) and Patrick Rabe (European Union), as well as the members of the DAC TWG who supported the research. The paper draws extensively from inputs provided by DAC TWG members.

The authors thank external reviewers who provided comments on earlier drafts of the guidance: Christina Stummer, Advisor Gender and Development, Austrian Development Agency; Christopher Demerse, Deputy Director, Humanitarian Organizations, Global Affairs Canada; Thomas Thomsen, Head of Humanitarian Team and Senior Policy Adviser, Ministry of Foreign Affairs, Denmark; Marianne Ronke, Senior Officer, Department for Development Policy, Ministry for Foreign Affairs, Finland; Giovanni Baticci, Senior Consultant, Africa Department, Ministry of International Affairs and Co-operation and Kadigia Mohamud, External Senior Advisor, Italian Agency for Co-operation, Italy; Jerome Elie, Senior Policy Advisor – Forced Displacement, International Council of Voluntary Agencies; Gaelle Pierre, Senior Labour Economist, International Monetary Fund; Yuko Dohi, Senior Advisor, Office for Peacebuilding and Reconstruction Infrastructure, Japan International Cooperation Agency; Omar Nuseir, Senior Co-ordinator, Humanitarian Relief and Co-ordination Unit, Ministry of Planning and International Co-operation, Jordan; Stein Erik Horjen, Senior Adviser, Department for Economic Development, Gender and Governance, Norwegian Agency for Development Cooperation; Raphael Shilhav, European Union Migration Policy Advisor, Oxfam International; Ahmed Said, Senior Government Advisor on Forced Displacement, Somalia; Tommy Löfgren, Department for International Development Cooperation, Ministry of Foreign Affairs and Ulla Andrén, Head of Division, Migration and Development, Department for Asia, Middle East and Humanitarian Assistance, Swedish International Development Cooperation Agency; Yahya Gülseven and Salih Yurç, Experts at the Turkish Cooperation and Coordination Agency; Glaucia Boyer, Policy Specialist, Partnerships, Migration and Displacement, Sustainable Development Cluster, United Nations Development Programme; Preeta Law, Deputy Director, Division of International Protection, Jackie Keegan, Head of Comprehensive Solutions Unit, Betsy Lippman, Head of Solutions Unit, Ewen Macleod, Head of Development Unit and Tammi Sharpe, Senior Advisor (Development and Solutions), UN Refugee Agency; Barbara Lecq, Humanitarian Adviser, Protracted Crisis Hub, Department for International Development, United Kingdom; Nicole Shepardson and J. Paul Reid, Office of Policy and Resource Planning, Bureau of Population, Refugees, and Migration, U.S. Department of State; Jakob Kopperud, Advisor, International Affairs, Europe and Multilateral Organisations, World Bank Group; and Manisha Thomas and Héloïse Ruaudel, independent consultants on forced displacement.

The authors would also like to thank other OECD staff who contributed to improving this guidance at various stages of drafting: Susanna Morrison-Métois, Anna Piccinni, Rachel Scott, Cyprien Fabre, Hugh Macleman, and Sarah Willis. In addition, the authors would like to thank Amy Hong, who served as editor, and Juria Young of Petit Four Design Ltd, the graphic designer and typesetter.

Table of contents

Acronyms and abbreviations

3RP	Regional Refugee & Resilience Plan
4Rs	Repatriation, reintegration, rehabilitation and reconstruction
ACAPs	Assessment Capacities Project
AIMS	Aid Information Management System
ALNAP	Active Learning Network for Accountability and Performance in Humanitarian Action
AVRR	Assisted Voluntary Returns and Reintegration
BPRM	Bureau of Population, Refugees, and Migration (United States)
BRACE	Building Resilience and Adaptation to Climate Extremes and Disasters
CALL	Syria Coordinated Accountability and Lesson Learning
CaLP	Cash Learning Partnership
CERF	Central Emergency Response Fund
CGAP	Consultative Group to Assist the Poor
CIREFCA	International Conference on Central American Refugees
CPA	Country Programme Aid
CRRF	Comprehensive Refugee Response Framework
CSO	Civil society organisation
DAC	Development Assistance Committee
Danida	Danish International Development Agency
DEReC	DAC Network on Development Evaluation Resource Centre
DFID	Department for International Development (United Kingdom)
DIAL	Digital Impact Alliance
DRC	Democratic Republic of the Congo
ECHO	Directorate-General for European Civil Protection and Humanitarian Aid Operations
EU	European Union
EvalNet	DAC Network on Development Evaluation
FTS	Financial Tracking Service (OCHA)
HFTT	Humanitarian Financing Task Team (IASC)
HIP	Humanitarian Implementation Plan (ECHO)
IASC	Inter-Agency Standing Committee
IATI	International Aid Transparency Initiative
ICARA	International Conference on Assistance to Refugees in Africa
IDA	International Development Association
IDMC	Internal Displacement Monitoring Centre
IDP	Internally displaced person
INCAF	International Network on Conflict and Security
IOM	International Organization for Migration
JEEAR	Joint Evaluation of Emergency Assistance to Rwanda
JIPS	Joint IDP Profiling Services
LCAs	Local Council Administrations
LGBTI	Lesbian, gay, bi-sexual, transgender and intersex
LRRD	Linking relief, rehabilitation and development
MENA	Middle East and North Africa

MFA	Ministry of Foreign Affairs
NDP	National development plan
NGO	Non-governmental organisation
NRC	Norwegian Refugee Council
NSAG	Non-State Armed Group
OCHA	United Nations Office for the Coordination of Humanitarian Affairs
ODA	Official development assistance
ODI	Overseas Development Institute
OECD	Organisation for Economic Co-operation and Development
PRMN	Somalia Protection and Return Monitoring Network
PRS	Poverty Reduction Strategies
RSA	Resilience Systems Analysis
SAVE	Secure Access in Volatile Environments
SDG	Sustainable Development Goal
SGBV	Sexual and gender-based violence
Sida	Swedish International Development Cooperation Agency
SNAP	Syria Needs Analysis Project
TacOps	Cisco Tactical Operations
TANCOSS	Tanzania Comprehensive Solutions Strategy
TOSSD	Total Official Support for Sustainable Development
UN	United Nations
UNDP	United Nations Development Programme
UNHCR	Office of the United Nations High Commissioner for Refugees
UNICEF	United Nations Children's Fund
WASH	Water, sanitation and hygiene
WFP	World Food Programme
WHS	World Humanitarian Summit

Executive summary

Despite the increasingly protracted nature of forced displacement, development policymakers and practitioners have tended to overlook the longevity of displacement. Providers of development co-operation have long viewed forced displacement primarily as an emergency humanitarian issue and the focus of the international community has predominantly been on addressing the immediate protection and short-term humanitarian needs of forcibly displaced persons.

In situations of forced displacement, resource allocation based on humanitarian needs continues to be a grounding principle for many donors. However, many other factors also play a part in donor decision-making, including domestic politics and wider strategic considerations related to foreign, security, trade and economic policies. Domestic actors may approach their engagement in contexts of forced displacement from perspectives ranging from conflict prevention to governance to migration management. Geographic proximity may also influence aid allocation decisions, with donors responding more generously if they see themselves as "affected" by the displacement. In fragile or conflict-affected states, which often host large numbers of refugees and internally displaced persons (IDPs), donors may prioritise emergency assistance over long-term development programming due to perceived risks.

Recognising that donor policies and responses constantly evolve, this guidance recommends that donors operating in situations of forced displacement prioritise three broad areas of work, where they can best contribute to existing capacities at the national, regional and global levels. These priority work areas are closely aligned with commitments made under Agenda 2030, the Sendai Framework for Disaster Risk Reduction, the Addis Ababa Action Agenda, the Grand Bargain and the New York Declaration for Refugees and Migrants. They provide a foundation for joint action and collaboration between development and humanitarian actors and focus on:

- **Strengthening co-ordination by creating a shared space where both development and humanitarian actors can co-exist.** Donor financing can create incentives for improved co-ordination between development and humanitarian actors built on a common understanding of the needs on the ground and an awareness of each other's priorities and commitments. Donors must review their own institutional barriers to coherence across aid and policy instruments, in order to promote the systemic and institutional policy reform needed to support coherent programming, transparency and accountability. Traditional donors must also recognise the interests of emerging donors, and their role in re-shaping models of assistance.

- **Enhancing the capacity and willingness of states to meet their responsibilities to protect and find solutions for refugees and IDPs, including through the integration of responses to forced displacement into regional, national and local development plans.** By advocating for, and supporting the formulation and implementation of national policy, legislative and institutional frameworks for forced displacement, donors can strengthen government capacity to integrate refugees and IDPs into development strategies and plans. Donors should support inclusive and flexible development programming that allows states and their development partners to adjust the scope of their interventions to respond to the emerging needs of displaced, returnee and host populations.

- **Supporting inclusive, durable and resilience-driven solutions that build upon the potential for displaced people and their host communities to contribute to local growth, recovery and development.** Given the increasingly protracted nature of displacement, and its impact on host communities and countries, donors should focus their efforts on interventions that build capacity within host communities, improve the self-reliance and resilience of affected populations, enhance access to comprehensive durable solutions, and advance principles of responsibility-sharing at the global level.

Development donors have access to government actors and economic policymakers who are not traditional counterparts for humanitarian agencies, and can use their convening power to expand better partnerships. They can fund quality analysis to support evidence-based programming and provide financial resources with the medium-term perspective needed to drive comprehensive solutions. They can direct financing to strengthen national institutions and leverage private sector response to support the inclusion of displaced populations into national systems.

With this in mind, the guidance identifies twelve actions, grouped under four key principles, outlining what donors can do to reinforce the capacities of key actors to advance comprehensive solutions for refugees and IDPs at the national, regional and global levels. The four key principles include: (1) **increasing understanding** through context analysis, assessing and managing risk, and prioritisation; (2) **learning through evidence** by institutionalising learning from failure and translating knowledge into practice; (3) **strengthening partnerships** by prioritising capacity building and supporting people-centred and value-driven partnerships; and (4) **delivering the "right"** finance by ensuring predictability, alignment and accountability.

Increasing understanding

Donors should build and adapt knowledge and situational awareness to facilitate flexible and context-specific programming – including who to work with, how to assess and manage risk, and how and where to target development co-operation to benefit forcibly displaced populations.

Learning through evidence

Donors should formalise learning, advocate for and contribute to improving the evidence base, and ensure that lessons learnt are accurately captured, communicated and translated into planning, programming and response.

Strengthening partnerships

Donors should encourage and foster community-driven and human-centred planning processes, support the capacity building of relevant stakeholders, in particular local and national partners, and invest in strategic and value-driven partnerships.

Delivering the "right" finance

Donors should strive to ensure a more predictable and cost-efficient response, by providing transparent and traceable funding, investing in, and working through, national systems (where feasible and appropriate), and undertaking critical, independent assessments of what constitutes value-for-money.

Twelve actions for effective development support in situations of forced displacement

Increasing Understanding

1. Invest in better context analysis
Invest in new skills and staffing and incentivise better knowledge sharing

2. Assess and manage risk
Improve the capacity to understand and anticipate different types of risks to facilitate adaptive programming

3. Ensure rigorous prioritisation
Make the right choices based on comprehensive context and risk analysis

Learning through evidence

4. Formalise learning
Invest in expertise, standardisation and innovation to support quality data collection and analysis

5. Learn from failure
Be transparent about challenges and opportunities. Identify what works and what does not work

6. Translate knowledge into practice
Promote data accessibility and use quality evidence to guide operational decisions and policy formulation

Strengthening partnerships

7. People-centred and community-driven programming
Support local actors at the national, sub-national and local level to participate in decision-making processes

8. Build capacities across stakeholders
Enhance donor field presence, incentivise dialogue, define progress and success in capacity building efforts

9. Recognise the strategic value of different partnerships
Adapt partnerships on the basis of needs, context and comparative advantage

Delivering the right finance

10. Predictability and flexibility
Adapt planning timelines to support quick reaction and encourage flexible budget management

11. Better alignment
Align funding with national development plans (NDPs) and work through national and local actors where appropriate

12. More accountability
Reinforce capacity to report on and track development and humanitarian funding streams

Bangladesh. Thousands of Rohingya
cross border from Myanmar.
© UNHCR/Roger Arnold

Overview: Development co-operation in situations of forced displacement

This chapter describes the context which donors should consider when setting strategic, operational, and programme objectives in situations of forced displacement. It highlights the challenges and opportunities that arise when working with refugee and internally displaced populations in new emergencies, established situations and protracted situations, emphasising that there is no distinct cut-off point or linear progression from one situation to another. The chapter also outlines the legal and policy environment, which defines the parameters of donor engagement in situations of forced displacement. In addition, it presents five displacement settings for policymakers and practitioners to consider when designing and implementing strategies and action plans. It notes that the vulnerabilities and needs of displaced populations emerge in different ways depending on the site of displacement.

The number of refugees and internally displaced persons (IDPs) worldwide continues to grow and, in recent decades, their length of stay in host countries has been rising. Many forcibly displaced people live in a state of protracted displacement, unable to return to their homes while lacking access to durable solutions elsewhere. Due to decades-old instability and conflict in countries like Afghanistan, Iraq and Somalia, millions of people remain on the move or stranded for years on the edge of society as long-term refugees or IDPs.

The changing nature of conflicts including the actors involved, the resources that fuel conflict, and the impact it has on civilians, has contributed to making humanitarian crises more intractable and protracted. Pressures continue to rise in countries located in regions surrounding conflicts, which host the majority of the world's refugees. Multiple displacements are a regular feature in the experience of flight, with refugees increasingly compelled to move from one place to another in search of effective protection and assistance (Turk, 2016). Large-scale refugee movements to Europe in 2015 provided remarkable insight into what happens when populations do not receive protection or assistance in countries of first asylum and are compelled to search for better opportunities elsewhere.

Developing countries, which have some of the highest and deepest poverty levels and the fewest resources, host the largest numbers of refugees and IDPs. Although international attention often focuses on those who flee — refugees and IDPs — the majority stay behind. In an environment of violence and economic depression, they lose the ability to withstand even minor shocks and may subsequently be pushed into exile because their resilience has been dramatically eroded.

As cities rapidly overtake camps as sites of displacement, refugees and IDPs rely less on aid agencies and more on ministries, municipal authorities, the private sector, civil society and community groups. Forcibly displaced populations attend local schools, seek medical care in public clinics and hospitals, rent private housing, benefit from existing water and sanitation systems, and find jobs with local businesses. Governments increasingly face the tension of attending to the vulnerabilities of displaced populations while maintaining social cohesion. Where refugee or IDP numbers are large, pressure on local resources, basic services and infrastructure is felt even more acutely.

The need for humanitarian assistance is at its highest level in decades and is growing. Meanwhile, humanitarian funding and capacity are extremely stretched. While humanitarian assistance is designed to be stop-gap and short-term, humanitarian activities have expanded into recovery and basic service provision in protracted crises marked by widespread and unpredictable needs which exist alongside long-term structural vulnerabilities. Most displacement will persist for many years. Data from 1978 to 2014 suggests that less than 1 in 40 refugee crises are resolved within three years, and that the duration of exile is usually a matter of decades. The persistence of crises in countries with internal displacement is also notable. Countries experiencing conflict-related displacement have reported figures for IDPs over periods of 23 years on average (Crawford et al., 2015).

Recurrent and protracted forced displacement presents complex and costly challenges that we cannot solve with short-term, emergency approaches to assistance. The international aid community must therefore ensure that resources can effectively meet both humanitarian and development needs. Developmental responses are critical to addressing the needs of the forcibly displaced and their host or return communities, both in the immediate response and in the search for comprehensive solutions (Devictor, 2016).

Understanding the likelihood of protracted displacement from the outset should influence the shape and duration of national and international interventions

Development co-operation is increasingly promoted as a key element of a comprehensive response to large-scale forced displacement. The 2030 Agenda for Sustainable Development recognises **forced displacement as one of the key factors that threatens to reverse much of the development progress** made in recent decades. It includes refugees and IDPs in the category of vulnerable people who should not be "left behind", and encourages a shift towards targeting those who are the furthest behind, many of whom are often to be found in fragile and conflict-affected settings.

The Agenda 2030's promise to **leave no one behind** is pivotal for the inclusion of refugees and IDPs in regular development planning, and may contribute to addressing many of the drivers of displacement. The leave no one behind principle is equally important when seeking solutions, and attempting to prevent displacement: where ethnic, religious, linguistic minorities or other groups, or the regions where they are concentrated, are systematically excluded from development, the seeds for conflict and for flight are nourished, and the chances of people remaining, or returning, are significantly reduced.

Although the sustainable development goals (SDGs) include displaced populations in the framing paragraphs, none of the 169 targets makes specific reference to refugees. Nevertheless, each of the goals, with their focus on **equity and universality**, should serve as a basis for the integration of forcibly displaced populations in the implementation of SDG projects, policies, funding and indicators. This means ensuring that every individual, including those from marginalised groups like refugees and IDPs, achieves the **full package of rights and opportunities**. Agenda 2030 is significant for refugees and IDPs because it is **long-term, country-led and country-owned**. It emphasises the central role of governments and their development partners in ensuring that national legislation, plans and policies align with the SDGs and, in so doing, underscores the role of states in enabling the inclusion of refugees and displaced persons in national development planning.

Addressing and preventing forced displacement can contribute to sustainable development. States that are disproportionally affected by forced displacement will see their capacity to achieve the SDGs seriously diminish. Consequently, understanding how displaced communities can contribute positively to national economies can help to turn humanitarian challenges into sustainable opportunities. When able to utilise their skills and coping mechanisms, affected populations can contribute to economic growth, benefitting both the displaced and their hosts.

Ideally, a collaborative approach in situations of forced displacement requires different actions from humanitarian and development actors. It requires humanitarian actors to consider host country capacity and continue to protect and support marginalised groups that do not benefit from access to national systems and wider development programmes. At the same time, it requires development actors to find long-term solutions for the displaced, their host countries and communities of return through reinforcing the capacity of national actors to serve all residents of hosting, return and settlement areas. Meanwhile, as part of this collaborative approach, national governments would exercise strong leadership, set the parameters for development co-operation, and engage in and provide the space for humanitarian interventions.

An important step towards **building common responses to forced displacement** is recognising that forced displacement is largely a development issue with humanitarian elements. This understanding implies that while forced displacement necessitates short-term humanitarian action, it also requires complementary long-term responses that consider social, political and economic implications for forcibly displaced people, their hosts and communities of return (Harild, 2016).

This collaborative approach should not challenge the role of national or international humanitarian actors, the principles that guide them in any way, nor should it call for the assimilation of humanitarian actors into development interventions. Humanitarian and development efforts must be complementary but one should not be undertaken at the expense of the other. In situations where states are responsible for excluding parts of their population or for harming them, principled humanitarian action must be supported. Where possible, development actors must engage early and in a sustained way, coordinating with humanitarian actors to bridge the humanitarian and development nexus, so that crises end sooner and are less likely to recur.

> The goal of international development is to improve the social, economic and environmental circumstances of the world's poorest, most vulnerable people in a sustainable manner. The aim of humanitarian action is to save lives, alleviate suffering, and maintain human dignity with programming that adheres to the guiding principles of humanitarian action: humanity, impartiality, neutrality, and independence.

Iraq. Returning families rebuild their homes in Ramadi.
© UNHCR/Caroline Gluck

))) OECD

Development efforts in situations of forced displacement seek to effect change in constantly evolving, adapting and responding systems. Each displacement situation is a unique and complex system, which may comprise layers of new, old or multiple displacements; a mix of refugees, IDPs, migrants and host populations; a combination of widely differing needs and social and human capital amongst the displaced and their hosts; and a variety of support systems – sometimes international, often local and informal.

Co-ordinated responses in such situations require shared analysis and a common strategic vision, flexible financing components, and an awareness of the need for multi-faceted responses based on comparative advantage. There is no universal design for effective development co-operation in situations of forced displacement. The challenges faced will differ from situation to situation, and will require context-specific responses. One size does not fit all.

Understanding the context

Displaced people should be seen as potential assets for local growth and development rather than as a burden. For this to happen, governments and their development partners must understand that forced displacement is a core development issue and that, as such, it belongs in national development plans (NDPs), even if substantial ongoing humanitarian needs mean that humanitarian actors must stay engaged. It is particularly important for governments of affected countries to acknowledge that new situations of forced displacement may become protracted, and that they need to develop long-term policy decisions from the onset of a crisis (Harild, 2016).

> There is the interdependence between the refugee problem and the problem of development, an interdependence which comes to the fore in the consolidation phase, which in turn is possible only within the context of the total development of the regions where the refugees are settled. This is a fact that must be taken into account from the very outset. This integrated approach to the refugee problem and the development problem, this union of all forms of multilateral aid and eventually of bilateral aid, alone make it possible to achieve maximum economy in the use of resources and to avoid duplication and waste.
>
> H.E. Prince Sadruddin Aga Khan, UN High Commissioner for Refugees, speech to the UN General Assembly, 20 November, 1967

Forced displacement has not concretely featured in development planning for several reasons. First, forced displacement is a complex cross-cutting issue. It can be politically challenging to bring together diverse stakeholders with different needs and priorities to formulate a common position. Domestic politics, socio-economic constraints, and negative public perceptions can influence willingness to include forcibly displaced populations in NDPs. Second, in the case of refugees, they are not nationals of the country concerned. Third, the regional dimensions of forced displacement increase complexity. Donors therefore need a good understanding of domestic pressures in host countries, which may include severe strains on service provision, political considerations and security concerns. Furthermore, they should support collaboration and dialogue at the regional level with countries of origin, neighbouring and host countries.

The multiplicity of development tools used by developing countries can further complicate attempts to include displaced populations in development planning. Countries employ several different SDG, poverty reduction or development frameworks. These frameworks involve different stakeholders, agendas, time frames, sectoral and geographical scopes. Donors should work with host governments and development actors to support streamlined responses, while recognising that displaced populations may have specific protection needs that may not be fully addressed by wider poverty reduction strategies (PRS).

The lack of accurate and comprehensive data on forcibly displaced populations also has implications for effective policy responses and long-term development planning. Inadequate information makes it difficult to predict displacement and to develop contingency plans that could help address root causes and carry out preventive interventions. Financial data remains siloed and lacks transparency, hindering collective planning efforts (Forced Displacement and Development Study Group, 2017). Addressing information gaps through the provision of technical assistance and open source data would help to inform decision makers, assess progress and enhance the quality of aid.

The underlying question that this guidance seeks to address – namely, how the development community can better respond to situations of forced displacement – is not new. The link between emergency relief aid and broader development assistance has been a subject of discussion for many years. Its origins date back to the late 1980s and have at different times been branded in various ways: linking relief and development; the relief-development continuum; linking relief, reconstruction and development (LRRD); and early recovery.

In particular, there is also a long history of initiatives aiming to overcome the humanitarian-development divide in order to empower displaced populations, strengthen their resilience and harness their capacities.[1] The Transitional Solutions Initiative and Solutions Alliance are two examples of these initiatives as well as more recently the Comprehensive Refugee Response Framework (CRRF). The move of the United Nations Refugee Agency (UNHCR) from largely care-and-maintenance models of assistance towards more direct interventions to support self-reliance and livelihoods, and its policy on alternatives to camps point to efforts to recognise the agency and capacities of forcibly displaced populations, and to respond holistically to the challenges and opportunities of prolonged displacement.

To better utilise development co-operation in situations of forced displacement, it is important to learn from past successes and failures. The more one understands the linkages between forced displacement and development, the more evident it is that a minimum degree of collaboration and co-ordination between key stakeholders around shared objectives is critical.

1.1   The legal and policy environment

For the past decade, humanitarian needs have substantially increased, driven by a complex mix of conflict, climate change, water scarcity, demographic shifts and urbanisation. The root causes of forced displacement and the dynamics of such contexts are complex and unpredictable. There is a great diversity of underlying causes, actors, needs, opportunities, and responses. Responders face multiple challenges, ranging from complex operating environments, funding constraints and gaps in co-ordination, to reduced protection space and limited opportunities for traditional durable solutions.

In past years, countries have made numerous commitments that provide the foundation for impactful development co-operation. These commitments can also guide programming interventions and provide benchmarks for engagement with humanitarian and development actors in situations of forced displacement. The most significant of these commitments is the 2030 Agenda for Sustainable Development, which took effect on 1 January 2016 and is the first universal development framework. Seeking to build peaceful and just societies, and to eradicate poverty in all its forms within a context of sustainable development, the Agenda 2030 is for the people and the planet, and has the ambition to "leave no one behind." To fulfil this ambition, the inclusion of refugees and IDPs in regular development planning is critical.

To provide longer-term solutions for refugees and IDPs, we need to consider the level of resilience in affected populations, institutions and markets at the outset and during the crisis, and support financing that can build resilience in addition to responding to the immediate crisis (WEF, 2016). The Sendai Framework for Disaster Risk Reduction 2015-2030, which contains seven targets and four priorities for action, provides a road map for building resilience and managing risk. Meanwhile, the Addis Ababa Agenda for Action adopted in July 2015 provides a global framework for financing sustainable development, making a shift from funding to financing. It also links economic prosperity with people's well-being and protecting the environment.

The United Nations (UN) Secretary-General's report One Humanity – Shared Responsibility, written ahead of the World Humanitarian Summit (WHS), emphasised the need for a move from delivering aid to ending need. The WHS resulted in agreement on a so-called "Grand Bargain" to make aid more efficient and to ensure it is locally driven. It also highlighted the need for innovative financing. At the 2016 New York Summit on Refugees and Migration, meanwhile, countries committed to set new standards of shared global responsibility with regard to large movements of migrants and refugees and to adopt the Global Compact on Migration and the Global Compact on Refugees by the end of 2018. They also agreed on the CRRF, providing a tool to effectively address long-term displacement through support to refugees and the communities that host them.

1.2   Contextualising forced displacement

Situations of forced displacement are often unique and complex systems, which may comprise layers of new, old or multiple displacements. They can include a mix of refugees, IDPs, returnees, migrants and host populations.[1] Displaced populations and their hosts have widely differing needs and social and human capital. They will also often have a variety of support systems – sometimes international, often local and informal.

Coping capacities may evolve or erode depending on when displacement occurs. In slow-onset crises, people's resilience may erode gradually over time. Those who move sooner rather than later may be less at risk and their immediate and long-term needs often differ from those of persons displaced by acute crises, which can lead to the large-scale destruction of social and human capital.

Forced displacement settings also differ. Forcibly displaced populations may find refuge in countries with strong institutional and governance mechanisms or, alternatively, in fragile or conflict-affected contexts. In the latter case, the degree of violence, and the capacity of the state and its institutions to provide security, resolve conflicts, and enforce the rule of law, may fluctuate. Weak institutions are often unable to raise revenues and use them for the provision of services such as health and education; or to facilitate economic development and job creation. Sites of forced displacement are frequently envisioned as large, sprawling camps but, more and more, displaced people live in urban areas, intermingling with host communities but not benefitting from basic services and excluded from business and productive opportunities.

The presence of forcibly displaced populations can cause strained relations between the displaced and their hosts. Situations of forced displacement can also become the setting for human rights violations, general violence, crime and instability, and further displacement. The needs of forcibly displaced populations, and strategies for providing development co-operation or humanitarian assistance, will therefore vary greatly depending on the setting.

Forced displacement and children

During the process of displacement, children may be separated from families or caregivers. They may lack access to basic and specialised services and face difficulties accessing documentation in countries of asylum. Children, including unaccompanied minors, are particularly vulnerable to abuse and exploitation, including forced recruitment into armed factions, underage employment, sexual exploitation and underage pregnancy or marriage. Furthermore, displaced children can face discrimination and social marginalisation and may have difficulties accessing education, health and other social services. As such, policies around forced displacement and development should take into account the special needs and vulnerabilities of children and adolescents affected by displacement. Development strategies must also protect children's rights and ensure access to birth registration, education, health and other basic social services, regardless of their status.

Kenya. Life in Kakuma refugee
camp in northwest Kenya.
© UNHCR/Dominic Nahr

》》OECD

From the perspective of the state, refugees, IDPs and returnees may equal beneficiaries. While some states may willingly mainstream IDPs and returnees into their development planning, others may continue to exhibit reluctance in including non-nationals, that is refugees, in NDPs. Alternatively, in some countries, IDPs are exposed to violence and to various violations of their rights either by the state or by non-state armed groups (NSAGs). Under such circumstances, states may be unwilling to recognise the presence of IDPs or take steps to protect them. In other instances, IDPs might prefer to stay in, or return to, areas under the control or influence of NSAGs, who may protect them in ways the state is unable or unwilling to do so.

Donors must also always consider the specific **legal and policy context** in which strategies or programmes are to be implemented. Each country's law and policy frameworks will define the parameters within which refugees, IDPs, and returnees need to negotiate. In many cases, however, even where there are legal provisions mandating access to systems and services, practical realities, including discrimination, physical isolation, cost and the capacity of responsible institutions can prove unsurmountable barriers.

Efforts to promote self-reliance and integration by providing access to productive opportunities may not be supported in countries that have not acceded to the UN Convention relating to the Status of Refugees (hereafter "the Refugee Convention") or that have made reservations to the right to work (Articles 17-19). In some countries, refugees are treated as unauthorized migrants and cannot access legal status or work permits. Other countries may allow refugees to work but will restrict employment or residence to camps, far from sustainable economic opportunities. The Refugee Convention (and the 1967 Protocol Relating to the Status of Refugees) provides guidance on the obligations and rights of refugees. At the regional level, in Africa, Europe and the Americas, refugee movements have led to the development of legislation responding to context-specific needs. The Guiding Principles on Internal Displacement outline protections available to IDPs. Human rights treaties, local law and practice are also important for both refugees and IDPs. The recently adopted Resolution R205 on Employment and Decent Work for Peace and Resilience provides more detail on how to achieve economic inclusion.

Box 1.3: Gender, forced displacement and development

Achieving gender equality and women's empowerment is a stand-alone goal – Goal 5 – of the SDGs. Given their disparate social and legal status, the developmental impact of forced displacement may differ for men and women. Women may have less access to capital, social goods, and the legal means to protect themselves in times of crisis. Across jurisdictions, women possess differential legal capacities to enter contracts, face systematic discrimination in their access to employment, and cannot own or transfer property which can have negative implications on coping strategies and resilience (Aolain, 2011).

The focus on women and girls is not meant to diminish the plight of men and boys, and minority groups, such as those with disability, children and youth, the aged, and lesbian, gay, bi-sexual, transgender and intersex (LGBTI) populations. Responses to forced displacement must recognize that women, men, and other minority groups each experience violence and its consequences, differently. Women and men have differential access to resources, including power, in times of conflict. Upon displacement, the resulting socio-economic changes may also have implications on the specific vulnerabilities and needs of men and women.

Donors working in situations of forced displacement can support women's access to basic services and opportunities for economic self-reliance, and consider their role in reconstructing their home countries after they repatriate or return to places of origin. They should identify obstacles impeding women's full integration into national economic and social programs and work with host governments to overcome these barriers. They should also work with development agencies and multilateral development banks to develop long-term programs for refugees and displaced persons, and in particular, support efforts to make refugee and displaced women self-sustaining.

Donors should also recognise women as **agents of change and leaders** in seeking durable solutions to displacement. See for example Oxfam's '"We're Here For An Indefinite Period" on prospects for the local integration of internally displaced people in North Kivu, DRC.

OECD

Situations of displacement are not static events. They rarely proceed along a predictable path from displacement to stabilisation to durable solution. Contextualising forced displacement therefore requires an awareness of various characteristics of displacement, for example, the size of the displaced population, demographics (including gender and age breakdown), socio-political and economic dynamics, as well as an understanding of the way that responses influence or are influenced by different phases and settings of displacement, as well as awareness of the existing legal and policy environment.

1.2.1. Situations of forced displacement

Three main situations of forced displacement, based on temporal dimensions – new emergency, established situations and protracted situations – are identified and outlined in the table below. There is no distinct cut-off point or linear progression from one situation to another. Situations can vary in duration, and can co-exist within a country or area. Successive emergencies may trigger waves of displacement within a country or region, resulting in the secondary displacement of people already internally displaced, or of former refugees who have recently returned, or are attempting to return from a displacement situation. The following table provides a description of each situation. The column on potential responses outlines suggested actions that humanitarian or development actors can undertake, and that donors can advocate for and support.

Table 1.1: Situations of forced displacement

Situation	Description	Response
New Emergency	• Displacement represents a critical threat to the health, safety, security or wellbeing of a community or other large group of people • Displacement is ongoing or has just ceased • Many actors are present, particularly in large-scale, high visibility scenarios • There is limited information on displaced populations • Local and national authorities are often overwhelmed	• Rapid admissions and reception • Registration and profiling of refugee and host populations • Rapid protection and needs assessment • Rapid context analysis including risk assessment • Life-saving assistance, e.g. shelter, food, water and health care • Security and access to justice • Deploy staff with development background to complement humanitarian staff • Map key stakeholders • Map country systems to facilitate scale up of national programmes (where appropriate) in given sectors, e.g. health, education, social protection • Involve displaced, host communities, local and national authorities in designing response • Embed emergency response in local development plans
Established Situation	• Relatively stable population • There may be sporadic influxes of new arrivals, secondary movements or spontaneous returns • Community institutions may have emerged • The attention of the international community may gradually shift to other "hot spots"	• Comprehensive and regularly updated context analysis • Joined-up assessments and contingency planning • Continuous registration and profiling (through national systems where appropriate) • Life-saving assistance for at-risk individuals and groups • Advocate for improved national and local legal frameworks and policies for protection of refugees and IDPs • Embed responses to forced displacement into National Development Plans (NDPs) and poverty reduction strategies (PRS) • Support intra-governmental co-ordination and coherence • Reinforce capacity of local and national institutions, infrastructure, and communities supporting refugees or IDPs • Support activities that strengthen social cohesion • Identify and support opportunities for livelihoods and self-reliance, relocation or third-country solutions • Support to countries or areas of origin to facilitate safe and dignified return • Put in place monitoring and evaluation systems and adapt programming as needed
Protracted Situation	• Twenty-five thousand or more refugees of the same nationality have been displaced in the same country of asylum for five years or longer • In IDP contexts, situations in which the process for finding durable solutions is stalled, or IDPs are marginalised as a consequence of human rights violations, including economic, social and cultural rights • Prospects for peace are at hand – repatriation is a possibility	• Monitor implementation of national and local legal frameworks or policies for protection of refugees and IDPs • Support local integration (social and economic at a minimum, legal, e.g. acquisition of nationality where possible) • Expand opportunities for relocation or third-country solutions for residual populations • Support improved conditions in countries or areas of origin to facilitate safe and dignified return • Facilitate transfer of socio-economic skills, capacities and resources to country or place of origin, e.g. training certificates • Undertake post-repatriation planning exercises with partners, especially host governments (minimize impact of return, streamline facilities) • Assess and evaluate local, national, international responses at the national and regional level

1.2.2. Forced displacement settings

Vulnerabilities and needs of displaced populations emerge in different ways depending on the site of displacement. The table below outlines five displacement settings based on spatial dimensions and provides a summary of coping strategies, and some non-exhaustive examples of vulnerabilities that might arise in each setting. Donors should be aware of these elements, and consider them when designing and implementing strategies and action plans.

Table 1.2: Forced displacement settings

Setting	Strategy	Vulnerability
Within Affected Countries	Populations at risk may adopt coping strategies that include moving back and forth between home and a nearby location.	While they may still have social capital and access to material assets, these strategies can leave displaced populations vulnerable to conflict, lead to the erosion of livelihoods and make assistance hard to deliver. *Example: IDPs in Syria*
In Peripheries, Including Across National Borders	To avoid long-term displacement, some populations may employ circular mobility strategies that involve neighbouring countries, or regions within their own country that provide access to physical security. They may engage in periodic return, depending on security, or see proximity as an opportunity to keep open prospects of return. They may reside in formal or informal settlements, often on the periphery of urban, rural or border areas.	These strategies can leave populations vulnerable in situations where they remain on the periphery and do not have formal legal status to ensure protection and access to services. Frequent movement across borders may raise security concerns with authorities in countries of origin and asylum and may compromise their protected status. Their presence may exacerbate ongoing conflict, particularly in the context of premature returns, or where camps in border areas are used as a base for insurgent activities. Their presence may contribute to fragility of host populations, particularly where they are hosted informally and there are no mechanisms in place to address the socio-economic impact of their presence or where their presence shifts the balance of power between communities or exacerbates previously existing inter-communal tensions. *Example: Sudanese refugees in South Sudan*
In Cities[2]	Many refugees and IDPs look to cities for economic opportunities that may be restricted in camps or rural settings.	Refugees and IDPs in cities may lack legal status, leaving them vulnerable to arbitrary detention, extortion, eviction or even refoulement. They may be subject to higher incidences of human rights abuses, with women and children most vulnerable to domestic violence, sexual and gender-based violence and violence against children. Refugees and IDPs from rural areas displaced in urban settings may require additional support as they may not have assets or livelihoods skills. In the absence of adequate protection capacity, they may be more prone to exploitative and abusive circumstances, e.g. child labour, early marriage, or forced to work in the sex industry. *Example: Rohingya refugees in Malaysia*
In Camps	Many refugees and IDPs look to camps for protection, security and predictable access to humanitarian assistance.	Refugees and IDPs in camps may be further marginalised, or fully dependent on international assistance, in particular where they are required to remain in camps and prohibited from engaging in economic activity outside the camp. Insecurity can also be exacerbated, for example, when diverse communities are living together in a confined setting and have limited access to sustainable peacebuilding and social cohesion initiatives. *Example: Protection of Civilian sites for IDPs in South Sudan*

Setting	Strategy	Vulnerability
In Transit	Where opportunities for return or integration at the regional level are scarce, displaced populations may resort to secondary movement, seeking entry into countries where they believe they will have access to protection and assistance.	Displaced populations in transit may have limited access to protection or assistance and may be exposed to human rights violations, e.g. rape, sexual assault or abduction. Many rely on organised crime networks or smugglers to facilitate their movement. Some are victims of traffickers, who hold them for profit or ransom. Smugglers often target women and girls travelling alone and due to a lack of financial resources women and girls may be forced into having sex to pay for the journey. Clandestine entry enhances their vulnerability; some choose not to register or find it difficult to seek protection. *Example: Eritrean refugees transiting through Yemen or Libya (from Ethiopia, Djibouti, Somalia and Sudan)*

Source: Adapted from Zetter (2015), *Protection in Crisis: Forced Migration and Protection in a Global Era,* https://www.migrationpolicy.org/research/protection-crisis-forced-migration-and-protection-global-era.

Policies and strategies that contribute to better responses to forced displacement can also promote development. Where strategies do not consider the impact of forced displacement on development, and vice versa, certain policy objectives may become less achievable and may lead to unfulfilled development commitments. Donors and policy makers need to be aware of how country policies that may not seem directly related to forced displacement interact with the human development of refugees, IDPs and host communities (Hong and Knoll, 2016). For example, policies regulating access to land may influence the prospects for the self-reliance of refugees and IDPs, particularly where they reside in rural areas where livelihoods opportunities are linked to the ability to practice agriculture or pastoralism.

Supporting refugees' livelihoods and self-reliance in Ethiopia

Ethiopia is party to the Refugee Convention, but holds formal reservations regarding refugees' right to work and primary education. Ethiopia's national legal framework, the Refugee Proclamation of 2004, grants refugees some rights but restricts movement, residence and the right to work. Until 2009, Ethiopia enforced a strict policy of encampment for most refugees. In 2010, it began implementing an "out of camp" policy and, in 2016 in the context of the New York Declaration and the Comprehensive Refugee Response Framework, it pledged to relax its encampment policy, raising the number of out of camp beneficiaries to 10% of the refugee population.

Despite some progress relating to freedom of movement for refugees, Ethiopian law restricts access to work permits for foreigners, and rarely issues work permits to refugees. Refugees cannot obtain business licenses and it is almost impossible for refugees to establish their own enterprise. Work in the informal sector has also been subject to government regulation and in refugee camps, government authorities have strict regulations about the type of informal work that refugees can do. Furthermore, refugees are generally not allowed to own land.

A 2011 impact evaluation commissioned by the UNHCR and the World Food Programme (WFP) noted the severely limited income-generating opportunities available for refugees. The evaluation noted that UNHCR lacked funding to promote refugee self-reliance and that refugees were not included in WFP programmes promoting sustainable livelihoods, productive safety nets and school feedings programmes for rural communities in areas surrounding the camps. It also noted that major donors had "not vigorously lobbied for policy changes that might expand refugees' economic rights and thus durable solution.'"

Nevertheless, there have been some efforts to improve refugee livelihoods. Between 2012 and 2014, local authorities allocated 10 km2 of land to Somali refugees in Dollo Ado area for agricultural activity, with the aim of increasing household income for 50 000 refugees and host community members. The Ethiopian government is also focusing on efforts to support job creation through national compacts, focusing on the development of a series of industrial parks following the examples of Jordan and Lebanon. Donors include the United Kingdom, the European Union, the World Bank and the European Investment Bank, and the aim is to create 100 000 jobs, around one-third of which will go to refugees.

These interventions intend to protect vulnerable groups, ensure their economic wellbeing and reduce irregular migration. The objective of the Jobs Compact is ambitious, particularly considering the poor record of industrial parks across Africa on job creation. To reach the intended scale, the scheme will have to attract a considerable amount of financing from both donors and the private sector. The compact provides opportunities on paper to a limited number of beneficiaries, while the remaining refugee population continues to face constraints vis-à-vis their right to work, own land, and their freedom of movement. According to the UK Independent Commission for Aid Impact and the Overseas Development Institute (ODI), it is yet to be shown that the job compacts prevent secondary displacement. The ODI emphasises that livelihood support is addressing the symptoms rather than the underlying structural causes of poverty, including the lack of rights to formal, better-paid and higher-skilled employment.

Source: Ruaudel, H. and S. Morrison-Métois (2017) *"Responding to Refugee Crises in Developing Countries: What Can We Learn From Evaluations"* http://dx.doi.org/10.1787/ae4362bd-en.

Understanding the range of dynamics outlined in this section can help determine who needs protection and what type of protection or assistance is needed (or possible) in a given displacement situation. It can also provide guidance on which actors should or can be involved in the response (particularly where states bear a significant responsibility for the displacement) and what options exist for durable solutions, for example, when return to countries or communities of origin may be inadvisable.

Further reading

1951 Geneva Convention and 1967 Protocol Relating to the Status of Refugees

1969 Organisation of African Unity Convention Governing the Specific Aspects of Refugee Problems in Africa

1984 Cartagena Declaration on Refugees

Convention Against Torture and Other Cruel, Inhuman or Degrading Treatment of Punishment (1984)

Convention on the Elimination of all Forms of Discrimination Against Women

Convention on the Reduction of Statelessness (1961)

Convention on the Rights of the Child

Convention relating to the Status of Stateless Persons (1954)

European Union Asylum Procedures and Qualification Directives

Guiding Principles on IDPs

Inter-Agency Standing Committee Framework on Durable Solutions for Internally Displaced Persons

International Covenant on Civil and Political Rights (1966)

International Convention on the Elimination of All Forms of Racial Discrimination (1965)

Kampala Convention

Pact on Security, Stability and Development in the Great Lakes Region

UN Convention on the Protection of the Rights of all Migrant Workers and Members of their Families (2003)

UNHCR Guidelines on the Protection of Refugee Women (1991)

UNHCR Handbook for the Protection of Women and Girls (2008)

UNHCR Policy on Refugee Women

Universal Declaration of Human Rights (1948)

UN Security Council Resolution 1325 on Women, Peace and Security (2000)

Notes

1   In the New York Declaration for Refugees and Migrants adopted by the UN General Assembly on 19 September 2016, states recognized that refugees and migrants are different categories governed by separate legal frameworks, but that they have the same universal human rights, face many common challenges, and have similar vulnerabilities.

2   At least 59% of all refugees now live in urban settings, a proportion that is increasing annually. Nearly 70% of Afghan refugees in Pakistan reside outside of refugee camps in cities. Most of the 1.1 million Syrian refugees registered by the United Nations in Lebanon, in a national population of 4 million, are living in urban host communities rather than camps. The majority of global IDP populations are likewise located outside identifiable camps or settlements, and live dispersed in urban, rural or remote settings.

Works cited

Aolain, F. N. (2011), "Women, Vulnerability and Humanitarian Emergencies", *Michigan Journal of Gender and Law*, Vol. 18/1, University of Michigan Law School, Ann Arbor, pp. 1-22.

Crawford, N. et al. (2015), *Protracted displacement: Uncertain paths to self-reliance in exile*, ODI, London, https://www.odi.org/publications/9906-refugee-idp-displacement-livelihoods-humanitarian-development.

Devictor, X. (2016), *Forcibly Displaced: Towards a Development Approach Supporting Refugees, the Internally Displaced, and their Hosts*, World Bank, Washington, DC, http://www.worldbank.org/en/events/2016/09/15/report-launch-forcibly-displaced-toward-a-development-approach-supporting-refugees-the-internally-displaced-and-their-hosts.

Forced Displacement and Development Study Group (2017), "Refugee Compacts: Addressing the Crisis of Protracted Displacement", *CGD-IRC Brief*, CGD-IRC, Washington, DC, https://www.cgdev.org/publication/refugee-compacts-addressing-the-crisis-of-protracted-displacement.

Harild, N. (2016), "Forced displacement: A development issue with humanitarian events", *Forced Migration Review*, Vol. 52, Refugee Studies Centre, Oxford, pp. 4-7.

Hong, A. and A. Knoll (2016), *Strengthening the Migration-Development Nexus through Improved Policy and Institutional Coherence*, KNOMAD, Washington, DC.

Mathieu, A. (2017), *"We're here for an indefinite period." Prospects for local integration of internally displaced people in North Kivu*, DRC, Oxfam International, Oxford, https://www.oxfam.org/en/research/were-here-indefinite-period-prospects-local-integration-internally-displaced-people-north.

Ruaudel, H. and S. Morrison-Métois (2017), "Responding to Refugee Crises in Developing Countries: What Can We Learn From Evaluations?", *OECD Development Co-operation Working Papers*, No. 37, OECD Publishing, Paris, http://dx.doi.org/10.1787/ae4362bd-en.

Turk, V. (2016), "Prospects for Responsibility Sharing in a Refugee Context", *Journal on Migration and Human Security*, Vol. 4/3, Center for Migration Studies, New York, pp. 45-59.

UNHCR (2005), *Handbook for Planning and Implementing: Development Assistance for Refugees (DAR) Programmes*, UN Refugee Agency, Geneva, http://www.unhcr.org/publications/operations/44c4875c2/handbook-planning-implementing-development-assistance-refugees-dar-programmes.html.

WEF (2016), *Global Risks Report 2016*, World Economic Forum, Geneva, https://www.weforum.org/reports/the-global-risks-report-2016.

Zetter, R. (2015), *Protection in Crisis: Forced Migration and Protection in a Global Era*, Migration Policy Institute, Washington, DC, https://www.migrationpolicy.org/research/protection-crisis-forced-migration-and-protection-global-era.

Zetter, R. (2012), *Guidelines for Assessing the Impacts and Costs of Forced Displacement*, World Bank, Washington, DC, http://siteresources.worldbank.org/EXTSOCIALDEVELOPMENT/Resources/244362-1265299949041/6766328-1265299960363/SME338-Impac-Report_v8.pdf.

Annex 1: The humanitarian-development nexus in situations of forced displacement

ICARA I
ICARA II

- First and Second International Conferences on Assistance to Refugees in Africa of 1981 and 1984
- African-led initiative calling for burden sharing and additional development resources for countries hosting refugees and returnees – starting point for refugee aid and development strategy.
- Limited impact due to lack of additionality, highly earmarked funding, different perspectives on what constituted durable solutions (voluntary repatriation vs. local integration).

CIREFCA process

- Process around the International Conference on Refugees in Central America, 1987-1995, following the end of several wars in the region
- Recognised that sustainable peace was contingent on the successful reintegration of displaced people.
- Launched several initiatives to bridge the gap between humanitarian assistance and longer-term development, focusing on quick impact projects.
- Modestly funded micro-projects unable to bridge the gap between relief and development.

Brookings Process

- Initiative of UNHCR and the Brookings Institution, 1999-2000
- Focused on bridging the gap between relief and development, improving systemic co-ordination from the beginning, engaging in joint assessments and analysis, and preparing joint action plans and project evaluations.
- Limited by institutional differences, short-term projects vs. long-term sustainability, and inclusion and commitment of local population and governments.

Framework for durable solutions

- UNHCR framework, launched in 2003
- Development assistance for refugees – to contribute to self-reliance of refugees pending solutions.
- Repatriation, reintegration, rehabilitation and reconstruction (4Rs) – to support returnees and those living in areas of return after repatriation.
- Development through local integration – to support refugees and host communities in facilitating integration.

Convention Plus

- UNHCR-led initiative, 2003-2005
- Focused on increased engagement of states, more effective targeting of development assistance to support durable solutions for refugees, and strategic use of resettlement as a protection tool and form of burden sharing.
- Foreign policy considerations not taken into account by concepts of burden sharing and special agreements.

Transitional Solutions Initiative

- Launched in 2009 by UNDP, UNHCR and the World Bank
- Government, humanitarian and development actors required to implement durable solutions.
- Joint, area-based approach focusing on post-conflict and protracted situations.
- Key principles include national ownership, decentralised decision making and optimisation of existing set-ups through avoidance of parallel co-ordination structures and funding mechanisms.

Solutions Alliance

- Following the Transitional Solutions Initiative
- Promotes and enables the transition for displaced persons away from dependency towards increased resilience, self-reliance, and development.
- Partners with broad range of actors, shifting the focus from multilaterals to include donors, host governments and private sector.
- Seeks to address protracted displacement situations, prevent new situations from becoming protracted, and works through thematic and national groups.

New York Declaration 2016

- Outlines a Comprehensive Refugee Response Framework
- Focuses on multi-stakeholder, whole-of-society approach
- Specifies key elements of a comprehensive response to any large movement of refugees, including well-supported reception and admissions, support for immediate and long-term needs, assistance for local and national institutions, and communities receiving refugees and expanded opportunities for solutions.

Priority areas for donor engagement in contexts of forced displacement

This chapter describes the multiple international commitments countries have made that can contribute to new ways of working in refugee contexts. Drawing from these commitments, the chapter provides recommendations for three priority areas for donor engagement in contexts of forced displacement. It recommends that donors focus on strengthening co-ordination between development and humanitarian actors, identifies challenges donors face in co-ordinating their planning and interventions, and provides a template for mapping donor policy objectives and instruments at the country level. It also recommends enhancing the capacity of states to protect and find solutions for refugees and internally displaced persons (IDPs), and provides some suggestions for localising responses to forced displacement. In addition, the chapter highlights some key considerations for donors and development actors when planning for comprehensive durable solutions, focusing on the potential for displaced populations to contribute to local growth and development.

Countries have made multiple commitments that can contribute to new ways of working in situations of forced displacement. A review of key frameworks and initiatives that provide guidance for bridging the humanitarian-development nexus points to a number of recurring commitments: better **co-ordination** (through collaboration and collective outcomes); **inclusion** (with an emphasis on working through national and local structures, and supporting those structures' capacity building); and a focus on **solutions** (moving from a reactive, emergency approach to informed planning that meets anticipated demand and that supports the creation and use of opportunities for comprehensive and durable solutions). Through the 2016 New York Declaration, and its Comprehensive Refugee Response Framework (CRRF), member states have also committed to greater international **responsibility sharing and co-operation** in the pursuit of a comprehensive response to large-scale movements of refugees. The New York Declaration also advocates for a **multi-stakeholder, whole-of-society approach**, which draws from the strengths and competencies of national authorities and emphasises **solutions**.

> Effective international co-operation cannot be taken for granted. The UNHCR 1951 Refugee Convention imposes no obligation to respond to appeals or to resettle refugees. Solidarity and responsibility-sharing for refugees have been disappointingly weak. In the presence of mass displacements, there is often a tendency to rely on short-term protection measures. This may discourage refugees and the host community from investing in the kinds of skills that will help refugees to find a job and contribute to society. Ultimately, a balanced public discourse is much needed and produces potentially valuable gains. Of course, in these difficult times, such a discourse certainly requires courageous leadership.
>
> Angel Gurría, Secretary-General, OECD, Remarks at UN Summit for Refugees and Migrants, 19 September 2016

Table 2.1: Key Commitments Framing Priority Areas for Donor Engagement in Contexts of Forced Displacement

Framework	Commitment		
	Co-ordination	Localisation and Inclusion	Comprehensive Solutions
Agenda, 2030	• Coherent and comprehensive responses • Participation of all countries, all stakeholders, all people	• Promote peaceful and inclusive societies • Provide access to justice for all • Build effective, accountable and inclusive institutions at all levels • Broaden and strengthen the voice and participation of developing countries	• Build resilience of the poor • Empower and promote the social, economic and political inclusion of all • Promote the rule of law at the national and international levels
Sendai, 2015	• Promote international co-operation and common partnerships • Establish global information exchange platforms • Promote coherence of national laws • Establish government co-ordination forums	• Promote national strategies • Enhance collaboration at the local level • Empower local authorities	• Invest in people-centred multi-hazard, multi-sectoral forecasting and early warning systems • Promote the resilience of critical infrastructure • Increase business resilience and strengthen the protection of livelihoods and productive assets • Strengthen implementation of inclusive policies and social safety-net mechanisms integrated with livelihood enhancement programmes • Empower and assist people disproportionately affected
Addis Ababa, 2015	• Multi-stakeholder partnerships • Bring together development, humanitarian, peace and security actions • Global forum building on existing multilateral collaboration mechanisms	• Peaceful and inclusive societies • Social protection and public services for all • Strengthen capacities of municipalities and other local authorities • Country ownership • Strengthen country systems	• Enhance and strengthen resilience • Generate full and productive employment • Decent work for all • Promote enterprises • Provide social protection systems and measures with a focus on the vulnerable
WHS, 2016	• Demonstrate coherent and decisive political leadership • Collaborative approaches transcending humanitarian-development divide	• Reinforce, do not replace, national and local systems • Ensure more inclusive societies	• Address root causes of conflict • Promote respect for international law • Fostering self-reliance, resilience of refugees, IDPs and host communities • Equitable and predictable responsibility-sharing

Framework	Commitment		
	Co-ordination	Localisation and Inclusion	Comprehensive Solutions
Grand Bargain, 2016	• Enhanced engagement between humanitarian and development actors • Galvanise new partnerships • Improve leadership and governance mechanisms of Humanitarian Country Teams and cluster or sector mechanisms • Develop coordinated approach for community engagement, supported by a common platform for sharing and analysing data to strengthen decision-making, transparency and limit duplication	• Support multi-year investment in national and local responders • Incorporate capacity strengthening in partnership agreements • Remove barriers that prevent donors from partnering with local and national responders • Twenty-five per cent funding to national and local responders by 2020	• Invest in durable solutions for refugees, internally displaced people and sustainable support to migrants, returnees and host or receiving communities, as well as for other situations of recurring vulnerabilities
New York Declaration, 2017	• Multi-stakeholder approach • Shared responsibility • Co-ordinated responses facilitating co-operation across institutional mandates • Co-ordination between humanitarian and development aid • Coherence between migration and related policy domains	• Refugee response frameworks on development planning • Deliver assistance through appropriate national and local service providers	• Tackle root causes of violence and armed conflict • Foster self-reliance of refugees • Expand access to livelihood opportunities and labour markets

The guidance draws on these commitments to identify three priority work areas for donors engaging in situations of forced displacement: strengthening the development-humanitarian nexus, working through national systems, and supporting inclusive comprehensive solutions for forcibly displaced populations.

2.1 Strengthening co-ordination by creating a shared space where both development and humanitarian actors can co-exist

A recent study commissioned by the Danish Ministry of Foreign Affairs observed that humanitarian and development aid actors often provide assistance in the same contexts but work separately and in an uncoordinated manner. The study also noted that, at the most fundamental level, humanitarian and development approaches diverge insofar as they are rooted in different principles build programmes based on different evidence, planning and budgeting processes. Further compounding these differences, institutional mandates and political interests rather than the needs on the ground, often dominate the priorities of international engagement in protracted crises. (Mowjee et al., 2015).

> Be realistic. Shifting from a strictly humanitarian approach to a mixed one that includes development, fragility and humanitarian instruments can take years to implement effectively and to show results.

Displacement situations, by their very nature, comprise a large assortment of stakeholders with an overlapping mix of competing mandates, different agendas and organisational logic, and diverse capacities, usually operating in highly complex environments. Development actors may face challenges working in refugee or IDP settings as they lack readily available resources to respond to large-scale influxes, may have a limited presence in refugee or IDP-hosting areas, or may be restricted by the fact that remote and marginalised areas hosting displaced populations are not a government priority. However, they also have the capacity to plan and implement development-oriented activities, have better links to government development planning systems and strategies and can provide resources for longer-term programmes. Humanitarian partners meanwhile, are capable of rapid action and often have good contextual awareness, including an in-depth understanding of refugee and IDP issues.

Box 2.1: A model of coherence

The Regional Refugee and Resilience Plan for Syria (3RP)

The 3RP aims to combine a humanitarian response focused on alleviating the suffering of the most vulnerable, addressing basic needs and preventing large numbers of refugees from falling deeper into poverty, with longer term interventions bolstering the resilience of refugee and host communities, while also capacitating national systems. A 2015 interagency analysis on international co-operation at New York University found that the 3RP rationalised a wide range of alternative funding mechanisms within a single national framework, or national plans, and thus offered donors a menu of options to engage development or humanitarian resources and provided a model that "constitutes concrete evidence of integrated funding for protracted crises" (CIC et al., 2015). The Danish Ministry of Foreign Affairs, in a 2015 study, acknowledged that the 3RP is "a significant attempt to bring humanitarian and development activities under a joint plan" (Mowjee et al., 2015). However, it also found that in practice humanitarian assistance continues to focus largely on refugee populations while development activities are predominantly being targeted at local communities. The study also noted that "In the case of the Syria crisis, there has been insufficient donor support for the development financing needs of the 3RP and particularly requests for direct budgetary support from refugee hosting governments" (Mowjee et al., 2015). The Centre on International Co-operation 2015 analysis stated that approximately 75% of 3RP funding is invested in refugees and 25% in building local resilience or supporting stabilisation measures.

Source: Ruaudel, H. and S. Morrison-Métois (2017) *"Responding to Refugee Crises in Developing Countries: What Can We Learn From Evaluations"* http://dx.doi.org/10.1787/ae4362bd-en.

Lebanon: Improving water supply for towns hosting refugees. © UNHCR/Martin Dudek

While humanitarian and development actors have different objectives, counterparts and instruments in forced displacement settings, these differences can be a source of strength. By working together from the onset of a crisis, development and humanitarian actors can learn from each other and build synergies based on their respective comparative advantages (World Bank, 2017). Levels of collaboration will vary from one displacement situation to the next and not all stakeholders can be expected to achieve the same levels of co-ordination or, for that matter, to contribute equally to collective outcomes (De Coning and Friis, 2011). Donors should sustain engagement with international partners, including through the CRRF, and work with them to integrate refugees, internally displaced populations and host communities into national development plans (NDPs) and the United Nations Development Assistance Frameworks (UNDAFs).

Donors should assess the opportunities for internal coherence and promote systemic and institutional reform, with a focus on improving co-ordination across their own assistance and policy instruments. Donor co-ordination can refer to co-ordination in the international arena as well as to synchronising specific country strategies. Donor co-ordination should consider the harmonisation of procedures (such as developing joint arrangements for planning and delivering aid), but should also entail co-ordinating development objectives and policies (Sjostedt and Sundstrom, 2017).

Table 2.2: Challenges to donor co-ordination in situations of forced displacement

Challenge	Description	Action
Political Obstacles	• National interests • Bilateral agendas • Host government bargaining power • Conflicting strategic interests	• Consider added value of donor policies and strategies for host governments • Collectively map donor presence, strategies and policies to avoid contradictory interventions and positions
Administrative and Structural Obstacles	• Additional work load • Different administrative procedures (national authorities and donors) • Lack of an inclusive national development plan • Lack of capacities in national administration • Difficulties in data collection • Intra-governmental institutional architecture	• Allocate financing for co-ordination staff in situations of large-scale displacement • Develop regional expertise, even in locations that are not traditional focus areas • Invest in donor staff on the ground or in rapid deployment capacity particularly at the onset of an emergency • Advocate for a results framework that applies across humanitarian and development programmes • Support ongoing efforts to establish shared data platforms (intra and inter-governmental) • Consider organisational restructuring to support more holistic programming, e.g. Netherlands Department for Stability and Humanitarian Assistance • Promote linkages across governmental departments through weekly meetings, e.g. Canada's Sudan Task Force, and secondment of specialised staff • Ensure humanitarian and development programme managers can provide inputs into each other's decision making processes, e.g. Danida
Division of Labour	• Reluctance to discontinue engagements in a country or sector where donors have established relationships and aid infrastructure • Reluctance to accept leadership of another donor • Reluctance to accept responsibilities and resources associated with being a lead donor • High numbers of lower-value projects dilute impact of aid and threaten activities with fixed costs and are most efficient on a large scale, e.g. energy and infrastructure improvements	• Play a larger role in fewer countries, concentrate on fewer sectors within countries • Map and identify comparative advantage of donors • Seek donor co-ordination for projects that may otherwise be passed by as they are often not cost-effective at the scale that a single donor could support • Where appropriate, identify major donor with the implied authority to convene other donors

Challenge	Description	Action
Agency and Personnel Incentives	• Reluctance to co-ordinate efforts for fear of diluting influence or "brand" in a country or sector • Legislators reluctant to give up control over direction of assistance programmes allowing them to respond to their constituencies • Fear that increased collaboration will mean less independence and that more efficiency will mean downsizing	• Create mixed teams working on development, humanitarian aid and peacebuilding • Rotate staff across humanitarian and development programmes and teams • Include collaboration as a key responsibility in staff job descriptions • Reward collaboration in performance assessments • Support joint and impartial assessments, planning, programming and evaluations in line with Grand Bargain commitments
Concerns About Direct Budget Support and Funding Pools	• Risk of misuse by recipient governments (due to lack of capacity or corruption) • Mechanism does not allow for adequate oversight by donors and their constituent taxpayers • The role of donor country non-governmental organisations (NGOs) that implement country development assistance would diminish • Some recipient governments express concern that direct budget support makes donors more deeply involved in core government functions, compromising independence • Donors pooling funds can create an imbalance of power	• Build, and where possible co-build, into the budget support process tools to improve data production and policy assessments on development objectives • Ensure that all parties have a role in programme design, implementation, and setting strategic outcomes • Manage risks by making "small bets", pursuing activities with promise and dropping others • Engage with decision makers at different levels of government • Consider mixed portfolio approach, e.g. direct and indirect budget support • Invest in local knowledge and meet regularly with well informed, well-networked people and groups in a given country to identify capable national and sub-national actors, and institutions worth investing in
Co-ordination Costs	• Additional resources (financial and human) needed to establish co-ordination mechanisms, sometimes for extended periods • Conflicting strategic interests	• Engage and collaborate with non-traditional donors, noting that while private sector investments, emerging donors, and philanthropic financial flows to developing countries present additional co-ordination challenges, they also present opportunities for a new type of collaboration • Invest in co-ordination instead of competing for workers, materials, or other limited resources. This will increase efficiency in a region

The following table provides an example of mapping of the policy objectives and instruments of donor governments in Afghanistan. It is not an exhaustive list but shows some potential interests and policies of donors. It illustrates a lack of coherence between some policies, for example, the promotion of sales of military equipment at the same time as an interest in the political settlement in the conflict, and the promotion of returns.

Table 2.3: Sample mapping of international responses to forced displacement at the country level

Donor government policy instruments and concerns in situations of forced displacement: The case of Afghanistan						
	Foreign Affairs	Trade and Investment	Human Rights	Refugees, Returnees and IDPs	Development Co-operation	
					Development	Humanitarian
Interests and Concerns	• Political settlement to the conflict • Regional security • Combating terrorism	• Trade relations • Investment opportunities	• Promoting respect for international human rights and rule of law	• Preventing additional internal displacement or flight across borders • Preventing irregular or secondary movement of Afghan refugees and migrants to Europe • Facilitating safe and sustainable voluntary return	• Structural stability • Economic development • Poverty reduction • Good governance	• Responding to protracted displacement
Policies	• Support for anti-terrorism activities • Military assistance and security sector training, e.g. United States	• Private sector support, e.g. development of small to medium enterprises • Foreign direct investment • Sales of military equipment	• Monitoring respect for rights • Advocacy • Capacity building and training	• Immigration and border control • Bilateral agreements on return, e.g. Germany • Legal frame-works, e.g. law on displacement	• Provision of concessional and grant aid for infrastructure, health and education • Development assistance to support good governance	• Provision of basic needs and livelihoods support in conflict-affected areas

Source: Adapted from DFID (2002), *Conducting Conflict Assessments: Guidance Notes*, http://www.conflictrecovery.org/bin/dfid-conflictassessmentguidance.pdf.

2.2 Enhancing the capacity and willingness of states to meet their responsibilities to protect and find solutions for refugees and IDPs, including through the integration of responses to forced displacement into national and local development plans

Under international refugee and human rights law, host governments are obliged to provide protection to refugees and respect their human rights. Governments have the responsibility to not return refugees to a country in where they have reason to fear persecution. Governments also have the principal responsibility to protect their citizens, including those who are internally displaced and returned from refugee hosting countries. National legal and policy frameworks and the leadership provided by governments set the parameters for how the needs of refugees, IDPs and host communities can be addressed by development and humanitarian actors.

Policy dialogues with host governments from the onset of a crisis are crucial to defining long-term strategies and development plans. Development donors and actors should work closely with states to identify, prioritise and sequence interventions based on existing international commitments and national actors' own priorities and concerns. They can also work together with states to ensure that the material conditions available for forcibly displaced populations (e.g. housing, access to water and hygiene facilities, and food) meet their basic needs, protect their rights, and are designed to facilitate self-reliance in the longer-term.

> Donors should explicitly include refugees, IDPs, and returnees as target groups for standard development programming including access to justice, livelihoods, sexual and gender-based violence (SGBV), social security, community safety and security, local governance – and measure their inclusion through disaggregated data.

Donors can build more responsive states in situations of forced displacement by advocating for strengthened legal frameworks and policy reforms, and supporting initiatives for better governance to boost the impact of development interventions. Donors should engage with governments to encourage the creation of protection systems that remove some of the legal barriers displaced populations face. Otherwise, the benefits of development co-operation will remain extremely limited, regardless of how well programmes are designed and implemented (Fratzke, 2016). Influencing protection systems for IDPs, however, may be more complex due to the intrinsically politicised nature of most internal displacement.

Building the protection capacity of national and local systems (e.g. by strengthening the capacity of the police to respect the right of asylum and IDP rights) or strengthening the mandate and capacity of independent bodies with specialised roles (e.g. national human rights commissions) can induce states to bear more responsibility for displaced populations. In addition to enhancing access to asylum, safety, and access to justice for refugees and IDPs, building protection capacity is an important step in working towards durable solutions. States that are well equipped to deal with new or protracted refugee or IDP populations are more likely to work towards solutions like local integration (Miller and Lehmann, 2016).

Box 2.2: Localising aid

The support of the United Kingdom's Department for International Development (DFID) for equitable access to education in protracted crises

Deciding how to support equitable access to services in countries affected by protracted crises does not have to be a binary choice between channelling resources through governments or avoiding the state. While it is good practice to align interventions with a country's development strategy, the level of alignment and the channels through which resources are managed, must adapt to the context and existing fiduciary risks.

In **South Sudan**, DFID development programmes are increasing access to education for all. The education programme supports schools and provides cash grants to vulnerable girls to protect their resilience and help them pursue an education. It is implemented in close collaboration with the Ministry of Education and through a network of NGOs possessing both development and education expertise.

In **Jordan**, DFID's education programme will help the Government of Jordan deliver quality education for Jordanian children and for refugees in government schools and in camp settings. DFID's education programme has **shifted away from short-term emergency response funding to more sustainable and strategic finance in recognition of the protracted nature of the crisis facing Jordan**. The programme is supporting the Government of Jordan deliver on their commitment to provide quality education for all children in Jordan regardless of their nationality and transforming the humanitarian emergency into a development opportunity for the country. It addresses barriers to participation including development of a catch-up education programme for Syrians and Jordanians who have dropped out or missed years of schooling. It provides quality public state education and non-formal learning opportunities for Syrians across the country.

South Sudan. Teachers insist on education.
© UNHCR/Andrew McConnell

Development co-operation can mitigate the impact of forced displacement by supporting governance structures, including through investment in infrastructure and enhancing service-delivery. Capacity building can include training and technical expertise, as well as logistical assistance in the form of equipment or transport. Additional funding for national and local systems can incentivise the incorporation of displaced populations into NDPs and facilitate their access to basic services such as education and healthcare. Targeted support to host communities can strengthen their resilience and address the widespread perception of refugees as a burden, which may lead to restrictive policies. These interventions are particularly important in fragile states, which host a large percentage of the world's poor, and where the shocks associated with large-scale displacement can severely affect a country's development prospects.

When deciding whether to work through or with national or local actors, donors should consider what arrangement is best suited for the context. They should consider the type and extent of displacement, the level of capability and resources within a given state or society, and the level of cohesion between the state and the citizenry as well as between different groups of citizens (Zyck and Krebs, 2015). While working through national or local actors may not always be appropriate or feasible, responsibility for development and for the protection of forcibly displaced populations, lies with countries. Donors should seek to reinforce not replace national systems, by building the knowledge of governments, promoting national strategies and enhancing collaboration at the local level. They should simultaneously invest in more research on what works and focus on efficient mechanisms for channelling resources directly to national and local actors. The following table provides some examples of types of national and local actors working in situations of forced displacement and offers a non-exhaustive list of functions that can enhance the capacity of the state to meet its responsibilities towards refugees and IDPs.

Table 2.4: Localising responses to forced displacement

Level	Actors	Suggested Functions
National	<ul><li>Governmental departments - Responsible for refugees and IDPs - Planning and finance - Sector ministries, e.g. health, education, agriculture, labour, and lands</li><li>National NGOs</li></ul>	<ul><li>Co-ordinate response and have overall control of development and humanitarian policy while ensuring humanitarian space is safeguarded</li><li>Build networks across governmental departments to support whole-of-government approach</li><li>Support development of national standards and policies to guide response</li><li>Mobilise existing technical capacities and financial resources to support programmes</li><li>Undertake national protection (including gender analysis) and capacity gaps analysis</li><li>Support social cohesion through state-led public advocacy on the rights of refugees and IDPs</li><li>Strengthen or develop legal and policy frameworks</li><li>Include refugees and IDPs in National Development Plans</li><li>Support sector-wide approaches, e.g. education, health, roads etc., targeting refugee and IDP hosting areas and communities</li><li>Build capacity through technical support or secondments from development agencies</li><li>Use UN Development Assistance Framework (UNDAF) or the CRRF to analyse development challenges areas hosting refugees and IDPs, and develop joined-up response plans</li><li>Include refugees and IDPs in bilateral or multi-lateral co-operation agreements</li></ul>
Provincial and District	<ul><li>District administration</li><li>Local members of parliament or government</li><li>Security agencies</li><li>Civil society</li><li>Private sector</li><li>Traditional leaders</li><li>Non-state armed groups (NSAGs)</li></ul>	<ul><li>Co-ordinate response at the district and municipality levels</li><li>Translate national policies into operational directives at the local level</li><li>Arbitrate between different interests at the local level, e.g. those of government or NSAG representatives</li><li>Identify inter-community and inter-village needs</li><li>Advocate for access to affected populations</li><li>Integrate gender-specific services that recognise the needs and vulnerabilities of women and girls, e.g. sexual and reproductive health services, and gender-responsive water, sanitation and hygiene facilities</li></ul>
Local	<ul><li>Community-based organisations</li><li>Local leaders (formal, informal, religious and traditional)</li><li>Local security agents</li><li>Local Development Committees</li><li>Refugee and IDP representatives</li><li>Host community representatives</li><li>Private sector</li></ul>	<ul><li>Define immediate and long-term needs and priorities of affected populations</li><li>Facilitate access to affected populations and support delivery of assistance – note that gender, ethnic or socio-political affiliations may affect impartiality</li><li>Provide institutional support and technical assistance programmes that yield results</li><li>Support small-scale</li></ul>

2.3   Support inclusive comprehensive durable solutions that build upon the potential for displaced people to contribute to local growth and development

Donors should work with states and partners to improve the enjoyment of rights by affected populations throughout displacement, progressively moving towards comprehensive durable solutions. The progressive approach entails advancement towards greater enjoyment of all rights until a comprehensive durable solution is reached. Comprehensive solutions have legal, economic, social and cultural, and political and civil dimensions, each of which needs to be addressed for solutions to be sustainable.

Donors and partners should work together from the onset of a crisis to develop solutions strategies that define the long-term vision of a solution and the changes needed to achieve it. The approach should be collaborative, inclusive and participatory, involving a range of actors including refugees and IDPs themselves and – as durable solutions need time for implementation – with a multi-year commitment. The following table provides a framework for donors to measure progress towards comprehensive solutions and provides a non-exhaustive list of sample indicators.

Egypt. Protection, education, health and jobs.
© UNHCR/Scott Nelson

Table 2.5: Progressing towards comprehensive solutions

Dimension	Description	Indicators
Legal	Refugees and IDPs enjoy a progressively wider range of rights and entitlements. This may lead to the acquisition of permanent residence rights and ultimately to the acquisition of citizenship in the country of asylum.	• Freedom of movement • Issuance of travel documents • Issuance of residence permits and work permits • Documented citizenship • Permanent residency
Economic	Refugees and IDPs can participate in the local work force either through jobs or through self-employment, commensurate with their skills, and obtain a standard of self-sufficiency that is similar to the host country population.	• Right to work • Access to land • Access to financing or credit • Access to livelihood training • Access to professional licenses and/or work permits
Social and Cultural	Refugees and IDPs are accepted by the host community and state into the community without fear of discrimination, intimidation or repression, and are able to create and maintain social bonds and links within the host community, participating fully in social and cultural life.	• Intermarriage • Establishment of joint businesses • Access to community centres • Representation of the ethnicity or racial or linguistic group in national and civil society media • Access to national services, e.g. such as education and health
Civil and Political	Refugees and IDPs are increasingly able to participate in civil society, including in community governance, local and central government, as well as through election processes and public consultations.	• Participation in community leadership structures • Opportunity to vote • Inclusion in conflict-prevention and peacebuilding processes

It is important to assess when situations are "ripe for resolution." Some of the prerequisites for comprehensive solutions include: leadership to help identify, plan and move the comprehensive solution forward; the availability of one or more durable solutions that can be accessed by the displaced population; responsibility sharing by donors; political will or state leadership in countries of origin and asylum; and external factors that can help facilitate a solution, such as political change or peace processes. Donors can provide support to peace efforts by facilitating political dialogue.

> It is critical to have a clear understanding of the motivations and aspirations of displaced populations themselves before investing in solutions.

Realising comprehensive solutions for displaced populations will require increased transparency and clarity in the planning, implementation and evaluation of processes around traditional durable solutions like integration, return, reintegration and resettlement. When supporting returns it is important to consider the populations in return localities that did not leave, to reduce the risk of conflict between these populations and the returnees. Furthermore, indicators for successful return should not be based on the number of returnees but rather on the success of reintegration initiatives. Donors should also provide opportunities for complementary pathways in their support for comprehensive solutions.

Box 2.3: Durable solutions and lessons from the past

South Sudanese returning to their country

Numerous reports have highlighted tensions and potential conflict associated with the return of refugees and IDPs in South Sudan. A 2008 evaluation carried out by the UN Refugee Agency (UNHCR) cautioned against measuring the success of voluntary return programmes through the number of returns, as numbers alone were less important than the sustainable reintegration of returnees. The same evaluation noted that many returns were unassisted, which resulted in numerous unaddressed issues around land and tenure rights, particularly in urban areas. A 2010 multi-donor evaluation identified cases of conflict related to the return and resettlement of IDPs and refugees as a potential "flashpoint". It observed that over 10% of refugee returnees between 2005 and 2010 experienced further displacement after return. Land issues and disputes over access to water led to many local disputes, some of which escalated into wider conflicts. It concluded that donors had not done enough to support local governments and communities to address growing pressures around land issues. A 2011 evaluation of UNHCR's community-based integration programme noted the trend of returnees wanting to settle in urban areas where there were more services. This evaluation found many returnees were frustrated, in particular by a lack of livelihoods opportunities, and expressed concern that this frustration could lead to future conflict.

Despite multiple challenges, there have been some successes in voluntary return programmes in South Sudan. Cash-based and livelihoods interventions are providing immediate relief to programme beneficiaries. The international community should continue to learn more about what works in order to better support South Sudanese forcibly displaced by fighting in the short and long-term.

Source: Morrison-Métois (2017) *Responding to Refugee Crises in Developing Countries: What Can We Learn From Evaluations? South Sudan Case Study,* http://dx.doi.org/10.1787/3b2fd4cc-en.

Table 2.6: Planning for comprehensive solutions – What to consider

Solution	Description and Example	Considerations
Local Integration	Promote access to education, labour and economic solutions as well as opportunities for long-term residency and naturalisation *Naturalisation of Burundians in Tanzania* In 2007, the Tanzanian government, in partnership with the Burundian government and the UNHCR, adopted the Tanzania Comprehensive Solutions Strategy (TANCOSS), which outlined a plan for durable solutions for the Burundian refugees who had been in Tanzania since 1972. TANCOSS provided for the acquisition of citizenship in Tanzania or voluntary repatriation to Burundi. Almost 80% of refugees opted for Tanzanian citizenship. The close affinity of the groups living in the area of Burundi and western Tanzania (including ethnic, religious and linguistic similarities) and their historical mobility across what is now the border were important preconditions for local integration of refugees. The design of the policy was viable because the refugees had access to land, becoming self-sufficient and contributing greatly to the local economy. On a macro-political level, the key drivers of implementation of the solutions strategy were the exceptional leadership of the United Nations (UN) and the Tanzanian government, and the responsiveness of donors – that is, the availability of funding.	• Political and policy context in the country, opportunities available in the host economy, socio-cultural factors • Capacity and willingness of displaced populations to invest in livelihoods • Impact of displacement on the host community • Role of local authorities and municipalities • Provide evidence of economic impact of refugees and good practices in integration • Consider aspects of financial inclusion, such as access to bank accounts, savings instruments and remittance sending facilities • Invest in self-employment, including through innovative crowdfunding platforms • Consider prospects for self-reliance through land-ownership. • Focus on strategic urban planning – displacement or return may occur prominently in urban areas • Invest in advocacy, promoting rights and positive impact of displaced populations
Voluntary Repatriation or Return	Voluntary repatriation is the free and voluntary return to one's country or place of origin in safety and dignity. This implies the restoration of national protection and the ability to maintain sustainable livelihoods, access basic services and fully reintegrate into communities and countries of origin. *Securing durable solutions for IDPs in Colombia* In Colombia, rights and reparations for victims of the 52-year war were central to the peace process. Prior to the peace agreement, the government afforded various rights to IDPs, including financing for new housing, a small income, support for obtaining land tenure, other legal papers, and affordable health care. The government strengthened its efforts to provide accessible and up to date data on displacement, and services and the support it offers for IDPs through its Victims Registry. The peace agreement, which came into effect in December 2016, made provisions for inclusion of displaced populations, e.g. allocating special seats in the government for communities affected by violence and ensuring that the safe return of affected communities was agreed to by all parties of the conflict.	• Ensure the exercise of a free and informed choice and mobilize support for returnees e.g. through "go-and-see" visits, engaging refugees and IDPs in peace and reconciliation activities, promoting housing and property restitution, and providing return assistance and legal aid • Include populations in return localities that did not leave in programming to reduce the risk of conflict between these populations and the returnees • Include urban regeneration activities in planning for returns, recognising that not all returnees will go back to their places of origin and some may choose to go to urban areas, where they have more access to services • Indicators for successful return should not be based on the number of returnees but rather on the success of reintegration initiatives • Invest in long-term evaluations of return and reintegration projects

Solution	Description and Example	Considerations
Resettlement	Resettlement of refugees to a third country where they can enjoy long-term protection and integrate into the host society can provide solutions especially for refugees with limited prospects for local integration or repatriation, or those with specific needs who cannot find adequate protection in the country of origin or asylum. *Private sponsorship programme in Canada* Enables refugees to be resettled with the support of private citizens, NGOs, or other interested groups, e.g. faith-based groups. An officer at a Canadian visa office makes the final decision on whether someone meets the refugee definition and is, therefore, eligible for resettlement.	• Consider innovative approaches to expand access to resettlement opportunities, e.g. private sponsorship • Draw on lessons learnt from studies by the Organisation for Economic Co-operation and Development (OECD) on main challenges and good policy practices to support the lasting integration of immigrants and their children to inform the structure of resettlement programmes, e.g. support programmes for minors, skills matching, factoring employment prospects into dispersal policies etc. • A comparative analysis of resettlement practices among OECD countries can provide useful information on best practices, and contribute to cost efficiency and enhanced integration capacities
Complementary Pathways	Complementary pathways serve to increase the range of safe and regulated means by which refugees may reach sustainable solutions to their international protection needs. *Family-based mobility*, e.g. German Humanitarian Admissions Programme facilitates family reunification for Syrian refugees with their family members in Germany. *Labour schemes* e.g. Talent Beyond Boundaries initiative in Jordan and Lebanon, a "talent register" to facilitate employment for refugees in third countries. Over 4,000 refugees were registered as of December 2016. *Education programmes* including private, community, or institution-based study visas, scholarships, traineeship, and apprenticeship programmes, e.g. United World College Refugee Initiative. *Humanitarian Visas*, e.g. Brazilian scheme issues special visas under simplified procedures to people affected by the Syria conflict for travel to Brazil, where they may then present an asylum claim.	• Complementary pathways may offer permanent solutions immediately or contribute to durable solutions realized progressively • Can include a combination of temporary entry and permanent residence or immigration programmes, e.g. family reunification for extended family members who do not fall within refugee resettlement criteria; points-based and skilled entry or other schemes; and education and apprenticeship programmes, including those that involve community or institution sponsorship • Ensure that programmes providing access to complementary pathways meet the necessary protection criteria e.g. clarify the legal status of recipients • Ensure that programmes do not leave behind those who have the greatest need for protection, e.g. single female heads-of-household, unaccompanied minors or persons with disabilities

Further reading

Cash Learning Partnership (CaLP)

Council Conclusion on Stepping up Joint Programming

Emergency Market Mapping and Assessment Toolkit

European Parliament resolution of 11 December 2013 with recommendations to the Commission on European Union donor co-ordination on development aid (2013/2057[INL])

European Parliament resolution of 14 February 2017 on the revision of the European Consensus on Development (2016/2094[INI])

Handbook for the Protection of Internally Displaced Persons

Handbook on Housing and Property Restitution for Refugees and Displaced Persons

International Labour Organization Guiding Principles on the Access of Refugees and Other Forcibly Displaced Persons to the Labour Market

Internal Displacement: Responsibility and Action

International Red Cross and Red Crescent Movement Cash in Emergencies Toolkit

UN Office for the Coordination of Humanitarian Affairs, Breaking the Impasse: Reducing protracted internal displacement as a collective outcome

Promoting Livelihoods and Self-reliance Operational Guidance on Refugee Protection and Solutions in Urban Areas

UNHCR Resettlement Handbook

Works cited

CIC et al. (2015), *Addressing Protracted Displacement: A Framework for Development-Humanitarian Cooperation*, Center on International Cooperation, New York, http://cic.nyu.edu/sites/default/files/addressing_protracted_displacement_a_think_piece_dec_2015.pdf.

De Coning, C. and K. Friis (2011), "Coherence and Coordination: The Limits of the Comprehensive Approach", *Journal of International Peacekeeping*, Vol. 15, Brill, Leiden, pp. 243-272.

DFID (2002), *Conducting Conflict Assessments: Guidance Notes*, Department for International Development, London, http://www.conflictrecovery.org/bin/dfid-conflictassessmentguidance.pdf.

Fratzke, S. (21 March 2016), "Move past the challenges and pitfalls in development-led responses to displacement", Devex, https://www.devex.com/news/move-past-the-challenges-and-pitfalls-in-development-led-responses-to-displacement-87898.

Miller, S. D. and J. Lehmann (2016), *The Challenges of Building Capacities for Refugee Protection*, GPPi, Berlin, http://www.gppi.net/publications/human-rights/article/the-challenges-of-building-capacities-for-refugee-protection/.

Morrison-Métois, S. (2017), *Responding to Refugee Crises in Developing Countries: What Can We Learn from Evaluations? South Sudan Case Study*, OECD Publishing, Paris.

Mowjee, T. et al. (2015), *Coherence in Conflict: Bringing humanitarian and development aid streams together*, Danida, Copenhagen, https://www.humanitarianoutcomes.org/file/77/download?token=P99VgU7j.

Ruaudel, H. and S. Morrison-Métois (2017), "Responding to Refugee Crises in Developing Countries: What Can We Learn From Evaluations?", *OECD Development Co-operation Working Papers*, No. 37, OECD Publishing, Paris, http://dx.doi.org/10.1787/ae4362bd-en.

Sjostedt, M. and A. Sundstrom (2017), "Donor co-ordination or donor confusion? How disputed problem framing affects the prospects for aid harmonization", *Development Policy Review*, Vol. 35/S2, Overseas Development Institute, London, pp. 064-069.

World Bank (2017), *Forcibly Displaced: Towards a Development Approach to Supporting Refugees, the Internally Displaced and their Hosts*, World Bank, Washington, DC.

Zyck, S. and H. Krebs (2015), *Localising humanitarianism: improving effectiveness through inclusive action*, Humanitarian Policy Group, London.

Mexico. Family waits for asylum
application to be processed.
© UNHCR/Sebastian Rich

Twelve Key Actions to reinforce capacities of donors working in contexts of forced displacement

Constraints in adapting to new ways of working, and the associated challenge of translating policy into practice, are evident in forced displacement settings. Policy aspirations may be at odds with domestic political realities, institutional incentives, behaviours and standard procedures. This chapter outlines four key principles to guide donors' engagement in situations of forced displacement: increasing understanding, learning through evidence, strengthening partnerships and delivering the "right" finance. While these principles are not exhaustive, they provide a good foundation from which to begin to address the gap between institutional rhetoric and realities. They define "what" donors should do to improve their own response capacity, and that of their partners, to ensure protection and comprehensive solutions for displaced populations. Twelve key actions, relating to each of these principles, provide some practical guidance for donor policymakers and practitioners, seeking to design and implement sustainable policies and interventions for refugees and internally displaced persons (IDPs).

While there is now a better understanding of the role of development co-operation in forced displacement situations, there is still a considerable lack of clarity on how to best operationalise appropriate responses. This section proposes twelve actions, grouped under four key principles, which can contribute to the design of more effective development responses in contexts of forced displacement. The table below provides some examples of points of intersection between the key principles and the three priority work areas outlined in Chapter 2.

Table 3.1: Designing More Effective Responses – Sample Questions

Principles	Priority Work Area		
	Humanitarian-Development Nexus	Working Through National Systems	Comprehensive Solutions
Increasing Understanding	Has a joint multi-hazard context analysis been undertaken?	Has a stakeholder mapping of formal and informal actors been conducted?	Is the political and socio-economic context conducive to solutions?
Learning Through Evidence	Do aid evaluations include forced displacement as a crosscutting issue?	Has the capacity to absorb donor funds and implement an effective response been assessed?	Is there evidence of a feasible solutions approach (e.g. profiling) in the specific context?
Strengthening Partnerships	Are all actors aware of existing development and humanitarian interventions?	Are there measures in place to build local capacities progressively at all layers?	Are local populations in sites or countries of return included in planning for solutions?
Delivering the Right Finance	Have efforts been made to co-ordinate prioritisation of donor responses and funding allocations?	Does the government have the institutional capacity for planning, budgeting, implementing and evaluating?	Are there opportunities for multi-year funding that can contribute to long-term, solutions-oriented responses?

Principle 1: Increasing understanding

Making the right choices requires improving our understanding of contexts. Development responses to forced displacement should be informed by robust conflict, human rights and political economy analysis to ensure that they do not inadvertently do harm to vulnerable refugees and IDPs. This information should be fed in at an early stage of project or programme design and should clearly articulate risks, opportunities and challenges. Donors need to enhance their own capacities, as well as the capacities of all relevant stakeholders, to undertake context-analysis, assess and manage risk, and prioritise and sequence activities in order to enhance their efficiency and effectiveness in situations of forced displacement.

The "do no harm" principle is derived from medical ethics. It requires humanitarian organisations to strive to "minimize the harm they may inadvertently be doing by being present and providing an indirect part of the dynamics of the conflict." Such unintended negative consequences may be wide-ranging and extremely complex. Donors must also strive to ensure that they "do no harm" and consider both the intended and unintended consequences of their interventions.

1. Context analysis

In the complex and fluid environments that characterise forced displacement, finding time to "see the bigger picture" is difficult but important. Sometimes, especially at the beginning of crises, information is lacking and access to sources is limited. Decisions may be based on rapid assessments and taken with a **high-level of uncertainty**. With time, it is important to fill in knowledge gaps and ensure that long-term decisions are informed by more in-depth assessments. Donors must **find a balance** between quick response and a thorough and ongoing analysis of the domestic context and dynamics, including relationships between displaced communities, state institutions and other key players.

Donors should encourage a **"joined-up" approach** to context analysis, which should take into consideration three basic elements: structures, actors and dynamics. This approach allows for better awareness of the **long-term factors** that affect particular forced displacement settings, an understanding of potential **sources of tension** that might impact on relations with host communities or lead to secondary displacement, recognition of **opportunities to mitigate** the impact of displacement, and awareness of the **linkages** between different sectors and actors.

Table 3.2: Some basic elements of context analysis

Structures	Actors	Dynamics
Long-Term Factors that Define Forced Displacement Settings	Analysis of Key Actors[1] in Forced Displacement Settings	Trends, Triggers and Transactions
<ul><li>History and geography, e.g. contested borders, access to remote locations, climate</li><li>Security, e.g. regional instability, capacity of security forces, presence of non-state armed groups (NSAGs)</li><li>Legal frameworks, e.g. refugee law, labour law, land and property rights, access to justice</li><li>Political factors,[2] e.g. corruption, independent civil society, representative systems</li><li>Economic factors, e.g. markets, barriers to access, competition over resources</li><li>Social factors, e.g. social exclusion, tensions over religion, ethnicity, gender</li></ul>	<ul><li>Interests, e.g. what interests do actors have in relation to the displaced population and how do these interests influence their actions?</li><li>Relations, e.g. between the various actors and where these need to be improved?</li><li>Capacities, e.g. what capacities do various actors have to influence responses to forced displacement</li><li>Incentives, e.g. what kind of incentives will promote better responses to situations of forced displacement? What disincentives discourage engagement in situations of forced displacement?</li></ul>	<ul><li>Long-term trends in forced displacement (where relevant)</li><li>Potential triggers for displacement (local, national, regional)</li><li>Possible future forced displacement scenarios, e.g. emergency influx, spontaneous returns</li><li>Interests, policy objectives and instruments of donors and development actors, e.g. military assistance, trade etc. and their impact on response strategies</li><li>Opportunities for durable solutions (including institutions and processes that can contribute to solutions)</li></ul>

At the level of programmes, a more granular level of context analysis is needed, one that focuses on a particular geographic area and the specific displacement scenario. It should include an awareness of **other donor priorities and existing development and humanitarian interventions** at the sectoral level so that donor strategies can facilitate responses that complement, rather than duplicate, existing interventions. Donors should consult with Resident or Humanitarian Co-ordinators, as well as the Comprehensive Refugee Response Framework Secretariat or Refugee Co-ordinator in refugee settings and respective Cluster Co-ordinators in IDP settings.[3]

Donors should **invest in staff with analytical capacity at both headquarters and country level** dedicated to facilitating in-depth context analysis. Context analysis should be subjected to interrogation and interpretation by team members with multiple perspectives, including those with specific technical skills and those with operational and field experience. Establishing a **community of practice** can allow donors to draw more actively on staff with expertise in forced displacement issues at regional, country, and headquarters level and support the acquisition of new knowledge and expertise where needed.

2. Assessing and managing risk

In situations of forced displacement, donors should be conscious of risks that may result from, or impact on, their strategies, policies and programmes. **Strategies should not expose already vulnerable populations to harm.** The understanding of risk should be a shared endeavour across all key stakeholders, grounded in "country realities" and guided by in-depth context analysis (OECD, 2015).

Risks will differ from country to country and may evolve during the course of displacement. When planning interventions, donors should consider three overall core risk categories – **contextual, programmatic and institutional** – within an overall risk management framework based on "The Copenhagen Circles" approach originally proposed by the International Network on Conflict and Fragility (INCAF).[4]

Figure 3.1: Core risk categories – The Copenhagen circles

Donor **risk aversion** appears to be strongest where development agencies face strong domestic and reputational pressures; where their country knowledge is limited; and where organisational incentives create pressure to demonstrate short-term results (OECD, 2015).[5] Large-scale movements of refugees, the increasing politicisation of migration, and access constraints leading to knowledge gaps, contribute to the high-level of risk aversion of donors working in situations of forced displacement.

Adaptive programming responds to several key understandings about forced displacement: that donors may not fully grasp circumstances on the ground until engaged; that circumstances often change in rapid, complex and unpredictable ways; and that the complexity of forced displacement means donors rarely know at the outset how to achieve a given development outcome — even if there is agreement on the outcome. **Adaptive programming provides a useful framework for addressing risk in refugee and IDP settings.** For example, adaptive programmes can allocate **flexible funding** in broad categories to facilitate quick budget re-allocations to respond to new or changing needs. They can **embed learning** in all elements of a programme, help programme managers adapt outputs to changing realities, and **devolve power** to field implementers to enable rapid response to new influxes.

Donors must accept that **risks can become reality**. Risk taking in contexts where opportunity for higher return is envisioned must be encouraged and be part of any strategy. Assessing and managing risk requires **quality analysis and co-ordination**, both within donor systems and with external actors, to ensure all key players have a common understanding of risks involved in programming in situations of forced displacement.

Approaches to risk management can include risk avoidance, risk mitigation, risk sharing, risk transfer and risk acceptance, each of which can be applied in different ways to the categories of contextual, programmatic and institutional risk as outlined in Table 3.3.

Table 3.3: Understanding risk types in situations of forced displacement

Risk Type	Example	Action
Contextual Risk Risk of state failure, return to conflict, development failure, humanitarian crisis. Factors over which external actors have limited control	• Environmental risks • Social cohesion risks • Infrastructure degradation • Impoverishment of local populations • Exacerbation of exclusion • New surge in displacement • Secondary displacement • Protection risks, e.g. sexual exploitation, child marriage and trafficking	• Conduct geographic mapping to identify areas of higher vulnerability • Monitor changes in current growth rates, fiscal balance and public debt • Map interventions against existing refugee density, i.e. percentage of refugees to the host population • Identify environmental factors, e.g. climate change trends, drought, land insecurity
Programmatic Risk Risk of failure to achieve aims and objectives; Risk of causing harm through engagements	• Strategies exacerbate tensions between displaced communities and their hosts • State capacity is undermined • Dependency on aid created or increased • Assistance fuels situations that lead to displacement – adding to conflict dynamics and to the financial resources of those responsible for conflict • Reduced political and economic space for protection of displaced populations	• Build large networks of external informants to provide contextual awareness and feedback to inform programming and "do no harm" • Recognise the value of local networks • Be conflict sensitive, consider interlinkages between political processes, human security, justice, humanitarian response, development, conflict and fragility • Ensure business continuity by building in contingency financial reserves or incorporating pre-agreed trigger mechanisms to address risk • Integrate advocacy for rights of displaced populations into all components of planning and implementation, including the use of a gender-sensitive approach
Institutional Risk Risk to the donor agency: security, fiduciary failure, reputation loss.	• Domestic political damage – reduced legitimacy with constituency and citizens • Reputation and legal risks when operating in territories with sanctioned terrorist groups • Aversion to exposing their own staff to security risks and simultaneously also potential risks on reputation when these risks are transferred to implementing partners and their staff	• Provide technical support and capacity building to countries to strengthen their fiduciary procedures • Remote aid management systems where access is limited, e.g. due to security • Enhance security procedures, e.g. information-sharing on security risks between donors, implementers, government and local authorities, and community leaders • Ensure better co-ordination and information-sharing, with national and local authorities and affected populations to ensure they are aware of types and extent of donor interventions

3. Prioritisation

In the environment of limited resources and great uncertainty that characterises forced displacement situations, prioritisation contributes to effective development assistance. Funding priorities may differ depending on the **type and profile** of the displaced population, and the **situation** and the **setting of displacement**. The assessment of where and how to prioritise funding should consider **how a displacement situation might evolve**, e.g. whether additional refugee movements are likely (due to intensification of conflict); where are displaced populations likely to go (base on pre-existing community networks); and whether the market supply has capacity to catch up with demand (population profile).

While donors should seek to align to national priorities where feasible, they should also recognise that different stakeholders have different preferences in terms of how they prioritise interventions, beneficiaries, modalities of implementation and timeframes and these preferences may well change over time. For example, at the onset of a refugee influx, governments may support the provision of parallel services to refugees in anticipation of a quick resolution to the crisis, but may eventually request support for public services when it becomes clear displacement will be protracted. Host communities may vary on their preference for parallel or integrated services, but will want to ensure that assistance to refugees or IDPs does not come at their expense and is not better than the support they receive from their own state.

Donors tend to make individual (and potentially less effective) funding decisions. For donors to make co-ordinated, needs-based decisions on the allocation of available resources to different crises, and address the phenomenon of forgotten crises, they need accurate information on available resources, global needs, and on who is doing what (and where) in the donor community. Establishing **common planning and communication tools**[6] can provide early indications of broader funding decisions, enabling donors to identify where their assistance could add the greatest value.

Donors must remain aware of the priorities of different stakeholders and consider how their programming **might influence them or be influenced by them**. Donors should also consider how their own stated priorities, e.g. thematic priorities relating to women and girls, or security, will impact on the needs-based prioritisation of the humanitarian response. Partners may often prioritise certain projects based on their perception of donor interests, rather than actual needs. Making the right choices will require **resourceful and adaptable thinking** based on context and risk analysis – as outlined in Actions 1 and 2 – and lessons learnt, strategic partnerships and a mix of financing instruments to manage trade-offs between speed and sustainability.

Box 3.1: Actionable prioritisation

Using Resilience Systems Analysis to strengthen risk informed programming: The Swedish example

Between 2015 and 2016, with support from the OECD, Sweden undertook a resilience systems analysis (RSA) in eight contexts to strengthen risk informed programming, prioritisation, and greater coherence between its development and humanitarian programmes. One of the RSA's main objectives is to "identify and highlight complementarity between result areas and to identify possible synergies, thereby assisting in decision making processes and the prioritisation". After analysing risk and stresses, and their impact on systems; characteristics of the system's components; and stakeholder processes, using the RSA framework, a roadmap can be developed to identify priorities and possible sequencing actions to support three types of capacities within each system (absorptive, adaptive and transformative).

In the case of Syria and neighbouring countries, for example, Sweden had not previously developed a strategy. The RSA helped map existing stakeholders and areas of focus for Sweden with actionable prioritisations. The resulting strategy "has been subsequently recognised as best-practice by a range of actors including UN agencies and other OECD DAC members." In general, it also found that Sweden has "a strong comparative advantage in regards to gender equality as well as to climate and environment, which both represent good opportunities to engage with other institutional donors to strengthen programme implementation." It was noted that in most cases the RSA helped prioritize engagement at the beginning of strategy development but was more difficult to apply to programs already operationalized or in review – the RSA can be used in complimentary ways. Mainly, it helped Sida increase focus on vulnerability and resilience building in fragile contexts; and shape a roadmap that prioritizes short, medium and long-term goals.

Source: MacLeman et al. (2017), *Resilience Systems Analysis: Learning & recommendations report,* http://www.oecd.org/dac/conflict-fragility-resilience/docs/SwedenLearning_Recommendationsreport.pdf.

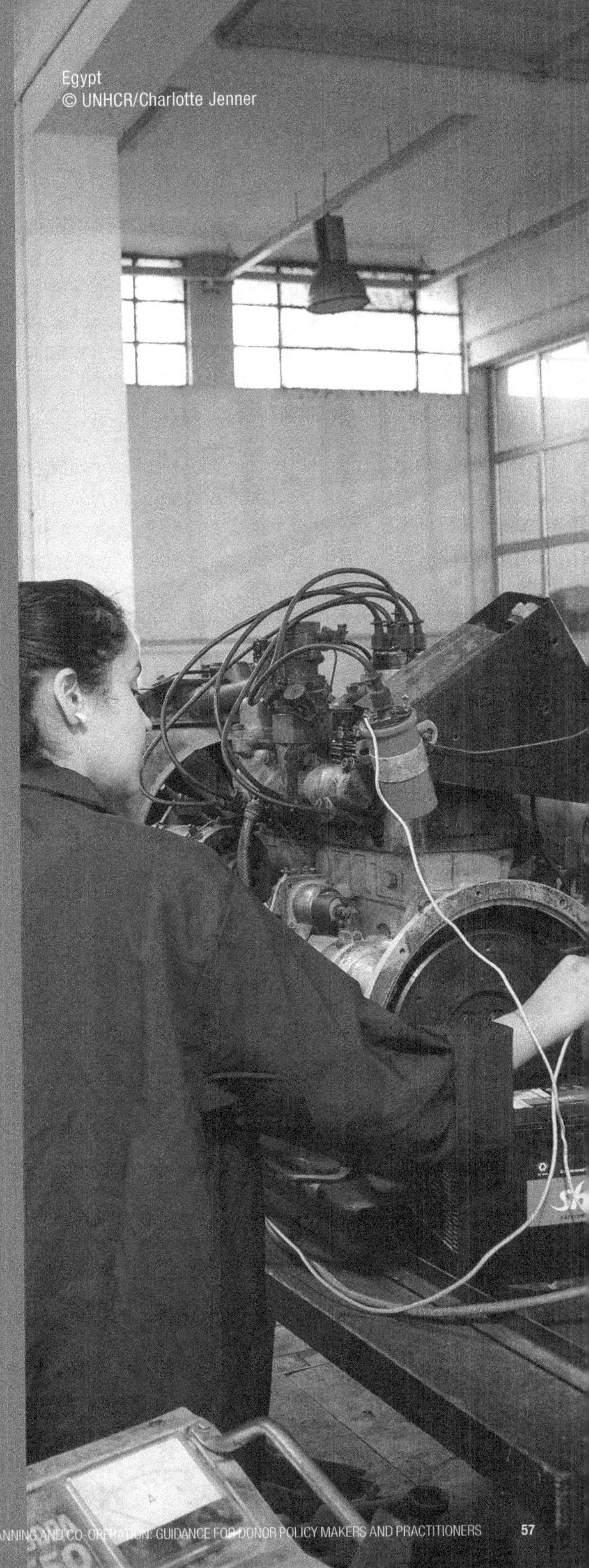

Principle 2: Learning through evidence

Responses to situations of forced displacement require comprehensive, reliable and comparable data. Donors, aid agencies, and host countries and communities depend on data to develop appropriate strategies, plan relevant responses and provide the administrative, personnel and material resources needed to address displacement-related challenges (Angenendt et al., 2016). Unfortunately, multiple data gaps exist in contexts of forced displacement. Good data are typically in short supply, particularly in volatile and hard-to-access settings. Even in settings that are not characterised by instability, the reliability, representativeness and generalisability of data may be limited by various biases, including selection, recall and reporting bias. Data collection may also be limited by the sensitivity of information required and issues related to identifying and accessing affected populations (Krystalli and Ott, 2015).

Ensuring accurate and up-to-date information on refugees can be challenging. Refugees may choose not to register, register multiple times or in multiple locations, be required to register with different entities or not be allowed to register at all. Statistics on internal displacement also remain weak and fragmented, as a variety of actors assume responsibility for data collection depending on the context.[7] Displaced populations may not wish to identify themselves and may be hard to identify, especially in urban settings, where they often have unclear legal status and may have similar ethnicities and socio-economic characteristics as their hosts (Zetter, 2012).

The amount of resources needed to produce meaningful, and methodologically sound data in refugee and IDP settings is extremely high, and technical or financial capacities to perform this function are limited (Jansury et al., 2015). **Many countries lack reliable data** on numbers of forcibly displaced populations or disaggregated statistics that provide information on socio-economic profiles and impacts. Internationally comparable statistics remain rare and future movements and displacements are still difficult to predict, which has serious implications for effective contingency planning (Angenendt and Koch, 2017).

For example, there is evidence that lack of data and poor information may have hampered some donors' ability to organise timely assistance in the Syria regional response. This was particularly true for donors without a field presence and without existing local partnerships. Donors that relied on partners' needs assessments faced challenges, as some traditional partners had limited experience or relationships with local authorities and country officials in the region. Evaluations suggested that weaknesses in forecasting systems, inaccurate or underestimated refugee flow numbers, and lack of existing data collection capacity also had a negative impact on some actors' ability, early in the conflict, to adapt their programming. Donors such as the Directorate-General for European Civil Protection and Humanitarian Aid Operations (ECHO) that tend to have greater humanitarian capacity, were quicker to open co-ordination offices and were better able to verify information, engage with key actors, adapt to the evolving context, and provide informed support to partners (Ruaudel and Morrison-Métois, 2017).

Where evidence is available, synthesising information and making it readily available to policymakers and practitioners remains challenging (ACAPS, 2016).[8] Issues of comparability of datasets and assessments may hinder their use.[9] Note that learning does not have to rely on new assessments; but may simply require that existing datasets – from national censuses to World Bank surveys and humanitarian assessments – can be easily accessed and combined (Development Initiatives, 2017).

Complicating matters further, **data may be politicised**, with pressure from various actors and agendas to come up with the "right" estimates (ACAPS, 2013). There is also a **gap in evaluation literature on the potential impact of conflict prevention, peacebuilding and state building on population movements**. In addition, very little knowledge and data are available on forcibly displaced populations who return to areas or countries of origin after crisis. Monitoring systems and evaluations should be encouraged to capture data on displacement, population movements, intentions for secondary displacement, and the possible impact of programmes on further movement where possible. Given the political importance of and attention to displacement, programme managers and development staff in member countries of the Organisation for Economic Co-operation and Development (OECD) should enhance the use evaluations to fill these gaps.

Working in insecure contexts often requires different approaches to data collection and assessment. In contexts such as Somalia and South Sudan, where insecurity limits the access of many international actors, there have been concerns about the reliability of data collected. One positive development has been an increased focus on using satellites, mobile phones and other information and communications technology solutions in efforts to improve information for better programming in these settings. A number of innovative data collection and monitoring methods have been piloted (see for example SAVE 2016 Toolkit of Technologies for Monitoring in Insecure Environments). Donors should continue to fund such initiatives to ensure that programming and funding decisions are based on accurate and timely information.

The Somalia Protection and Return Monitoring Network (PRMN)

The PRMN is a project led by the UN Refugee Agency (UNHCR), which acts as a platform for identifying and reporting on displacements (including returns) of populations in Somalia as well as protection incidents underlying such movements. On behalf of UNHCR, the Norwegian Refugee Council (NRC) works through 39 local partners in the field in Somaliland, Puntland and in South Central Somalia. Partners monitor population displacements and return movements by targeting strategic points including transit sites, IDP settlements, border crossings and other ad hoc locations. Data are captured by interviewing displaced persons (generating "household-level" reports) primarily at points of arrival or by interviewing key informants (generating "group reports") at IDP settlements, transit centres and other strategic locations. Interviews rely on the use of a standardized form designed to capture information on displacements and protection incidents. Household-level reports include disaggregated demographic data and family vulnerabilities. Sensitive personal information is not stored. Reports are uploaded onto a web-based platform after verification by NRC field staff, either in person or through third parties. Referral services and basic emergency support assistance are available through the network to victims and survivors of serious protection incidents. The PRMN provides real-time identification of displacements especially where catalysed by natural disasters (flood, drought etc.) or man-made events such as conflict. Procedures are in place for monitors to flag key events and issue "flash reports" informing the wider humanitarian community of displacements, the cause and wherever possible a preliminary indicator of immediate priority needs. The breadth of coverage of the PRMN, combined with the capture of origins, destinations and causes of movements, mean that the network can provide insight into displacements over a significant proportion of Somalia.

Source: PRMN (2017), *Somalia: Displacements dashboard*, https://data2.unhcr.org/en/documents/details/58901.

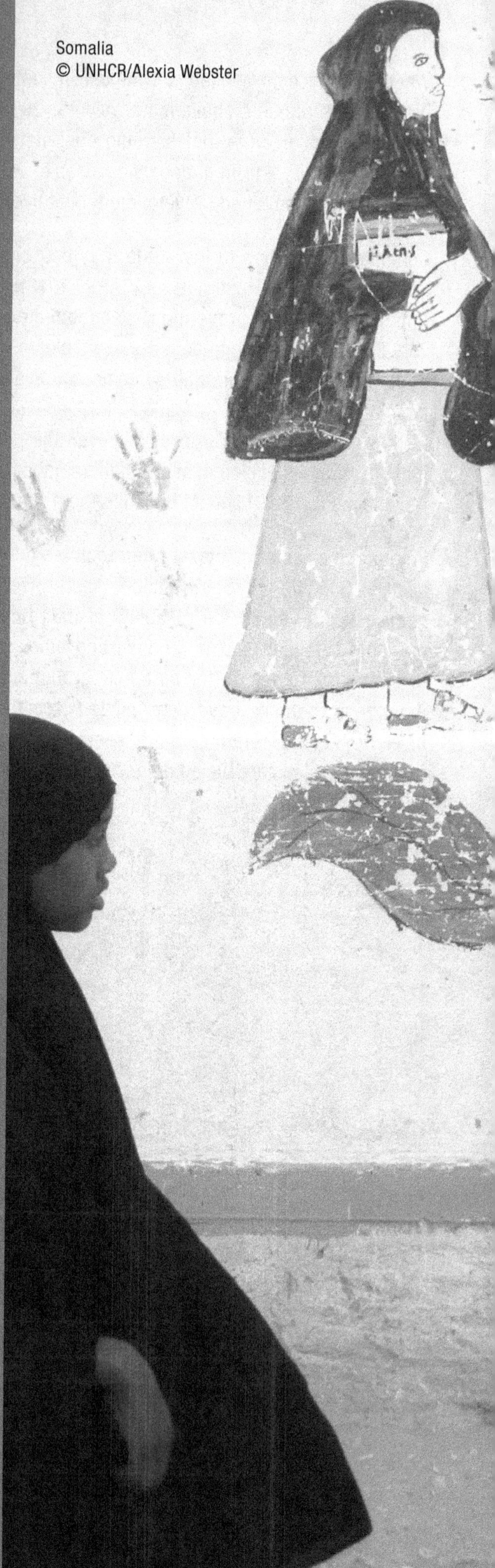
Somalia
© UNHCR/Alexia Webster

» OECD

4. Formalise learning

Donors should formalise learning by making **explicit reference** to the need for monitoring and evaluations in project agreements, and by ensuring funding is available for monitoring and robust evaluations of what works and does not work over time. Funding should also support strengthened expertise in data collection and analysis, with a **focus on national and local capacities** in line with the Paris Declaration commitments, particularly where donor policies and programmes emphasise on the inclusion of forcibly displaced populations in national systems.

Donors should ensure that their own evidence is **disseminated to relevant stakeholders** to mainstream learning processes. A 2010 study by the OECD Development Assistance Committee (DAC) Network on Development Evaluation (EvalNet) provided a mixed picture of communication with national actors on learning. Even when evaluation findings were disseminated to or in partner countries, this was done on a top-down basis with little involvement of partner country governments and other stakeholders aside from limited engagement with local civil society (Evalnet, 2010). It is also important to note that, while knowledge dissemination is important, donors and their partners should only share information after conducting a risk assessment and receiving informed consent from affected populations.

While recognising the importance of being context-specific when collecting data in situations of forced displacement, donors should continue to invest in and support efforts to **standardise data collection** questions, categories and thresholds at the international level, with a focus on providing clear guidelines on methods and process in unpredictable situations. Joint assessments and the development of shared outcomes can formalise learning, build trust among stakeholders and facilitate effective programming. The Internet is increasingly used for data management through online databases and platforms. Donors should promote these initiatives, which can be used to share evidence and reinforce efforts to derive lessons learned and best practices from programming. However, safeguards should be incorporated to ensure that privacy rights of displaced populations are respected.

Building Resilience and Adaptation to Climate Extremes and Disasters (BRACED)

BRACED is designed to tackle poverty, insecurity, disasters and climate extremes through scaling up proven technologies and practices in at-risk countries. Research and evaluation build evidence on what works on adaptation, disaster risk reduction and build national and international capacity to respond to climate related disasters. The BRACED Knowledge Manager Consortium, led by the Overseas Development Institute (ODI), aims to build a new approach to knowledge and learning. It acts as a centre for developing and disseminating knowledge and ensuring BRACED contributes to sustained impact beyond the communities directly supported by funded projects. Evidence from across the BRACED portfolio and beyond will be gathered through evaluations at different levels, thematic research, and original learning approaches. BRACED supports project partners to increase the impact of their work by integrating ongoing learning into their work. Evidence is shared with practitioners to benefit wider programming and feeds in to policy dialogues to inform national policies and institutions. By supporting better integration of disaster risk reduction, adaptation and development approaches, BRACED expects to benefit up to five million vulnerable people by helping them become more resilient to climate extremes. Fifteen projects operate across 13 countries: Burkina Faso, Chad, Mali, Senegal, Niger, Mauritania, Sudan, South Sudan, Ethiopia, Uganda, Kenya, Myanmar, and Nepal.

Source: BRACED Project, http://www.braced.org/.

Kenya. Water pipeline supplies new refugee camp.
© UNHCR/Samuel Otieno

OECD

5. Learning from failure

There are strong disincentives for honesty in the development industry. Donors do not like being associated with a failed initiative, particularly in the era of the results agenda. Admission of failure becomes even more difficult and sensitive when, as in the case of forced displacement, the initiative involves many stakeholders, ranging from governments to development agencies and civil society organisations (CSOs).

Donors should encourage **critical reflection and wide sharing**[10] of lessons learnt – both good and bad. Donors also need to develop effective and strategic ways of disseminating information. There should be clarity about **who communicates what**, that is, the role of the development agency in communicating results as well as what the government will report directly about development co-operation.

The aid community would benefit from **"safe spaces"** through which they can exchange lessons about failure, whether in the form of conferences or practice-based journals. By creating an environment where it is safe to fail, donors can build partners' confidence that failure does not necessarily mean the end of funding. **Creating more honest relationships will foster more meaningful partnerships.**

Donors make a difference not only through formal interventions related to objectives, but through the relationships and influence they have on others, the values they represent and spread, and how the worth of their intervention is judged by others. Donor impact should be communicated with less focus on results and more focus on the choice and quality of relationships (Eyben, 2005). With this in mind, donors should prioritise honest feedback, e.g. through regular social audits as a routine 360 degree-type process with their different stakeholders (O'Dwyer, 2005).

The Joint Evaluation of Emergency Assistance to Rwanda (JEEAR)

The 1994 genocide and the ensuing relief operations provoked an unprecedented international collaborative evaluation process – JEEAR – which has remained unsurpassed in terms of its scope and scale, and arguably its impact.

The JEEAR process was first proposed by the Danish International Development Agency (Danida) in September 1994, just two months after the end of the genocide and the influx of almost two million refugees into the Democratic Republic of the Congo (DRC). In November 1994, Danida's evaluation department organised a meeting of organisations interested in participating in a collaborative evaluation process. The scale of the process was unprecedented. Overall, 52 researchers were employed on five separate studies, and the cost of the whole process including translation and dissemination of the published reports was USD 1.7 million.

The reports found and communicated significant failures including: significant signs that forces in Rwanda were preparing the climate and structures for genocide and political assassinations were ignored, discounted or misinterpreted by the international community, thereby not only indicating an unwillingness to intervene, but communicating that unwillingness to those who were planning genocide; through hesitations to respond, the international community failed to stop or stem the genocide, and in this regard shares responsibility for the extent of it; the essential failures of the response of the international community to the genocide in Rwanda were political; improved contingency planning and co-ordination, increased preparedness measures and adoption of more cost-effective interventions could have saved more lives, as well as resources; and the failure of the international community as a whole to provide adequate support for the government of Rwanda has also undermined future stability and development efforts.

In 1995, the Joint Evaluation Follow-up, Monitoring and Facilitation Network, was set up to monitor and report on the evaluations' 64 recommendations. JEEAR's impact was found to be most evident in the areas of humanitarian accountability and evaluation. At least three of the significant initiatives aimed at improving accountability and performance in the humanitarian sector over the last eight years – the Sphere Project, the Active Learning Network for Accountability and Performance in Humanitarian Action (ALNAP) and the Humanitarian Accountability Project (HAP) – stemmed directly from, or were substantially influenced by, JEEAR. JEEAR's impact was far less evident in relation to the discourse on the prevention of genocide and in relation to political and military processes in the Great Lakes. In addition, recommendations on policy coherence were misinterpreted by some actors and seen by some donor organisations as a call for the integration of humanitarian assistance within an overall political framework.

Source: Borton, J. (2004), *The Joint Evaluation of Emergency Assistance to Rwanda*, http://odihpn.org/magazine/the-joint-evaluation-of-emergency-assistance-to-rwanda/.

6. Translating knowledge into practice

The development sector revolves around the principle that better use of research and evidence in policy and practice can help save lives, reduce poverty and improve quality of life. Yet, applying evidence to guide and inform the sector's many actors and to shape policy agendas is a difficult task. **Evidence, by itself, does not make decisions**. In most cases, decision-makers will need to balance different types of evidence, pointing to different conclusions, before making a decision.

Development programmes implemented in areas where there may be significant populations of displaced individuals, do not necessary include IDPs and refugees in programming or mention them in the subsequent evaluations. Development evaluations at the country level should be encouraged to include information on how refugees and IDPs are included in programming, national development plans and country level strategy. In general, there is often a missed opportunity for development evaluations to **include forced displacement as a crosscutting issue** in contexts where there are sizable displaced communities.

Despite repeated policy aspirations of using development assistance to address the root drivers of conflict and displacement, there does not appear to be strong evaluation evidence that these efforts are successful in the short term or that programmes focusing on education, employment and livelihood opportunities for the displaced, will necessary lead to reduced levels of secondary displacement. Root causes are multifaceted, context-specific and require different strategic responses by states. Detailed analyses must inform all initiatives addressing the root causes of displacement and form the basis of all support to countries of origin.

Donors need to have a **clear vision of the goals** of their learning strategies (both at the organisational and individual level), examine how they **collect and deliver learning**, and assess how to **integrate learning** into all stages of the project cycle. They should be able to clearly identify returns from investment in learning so as to assess whether and how learning contributes to decision making.

Box 3.6: Promoting evidence-based decision making in displacement situations

The Joint IDP Profiling Service (JIPS)

In order to provide appropriate assistance, protection and solutions for forcibly displaced people, it is important to know who they are and what their specific needs and capacities are. JIPS is an inter-agency service which aims to support government, humanitarian and development actors to design and implement collaborative profiling exercises. In 2017, it was funded by the U.S. Department of State's Bureau of Population, Refugees, and Migration, Danida, the Danish Refugee Council, the Norwegian Ministry of Foreign Affairs, the Office of U.S. Foreign Disaster Assistance and the UNHCR.

Working primarily in situations of internal displacement, the service seeks to promote a culture of evidence-based decision making in displacement situations. Provided both on-site and remotely, JIPS tailors its support to the needs on the ground and enhances in-country profiling and capacity building to generate locally owned, impactful and agreed-upon data. Profiling exercises collect data disaggregated by sex, age, location and diversity. Once analysed, these data become the evidence base for decision making, securing funds and designing policies that ensure sustainable solutions for displaced people. JIPS supports a collaborative approach to profiling. While profiling is a resource-intensive and often very challenging exercise, the data collected provide insight into the lives of people affected by displacement – including host populations.

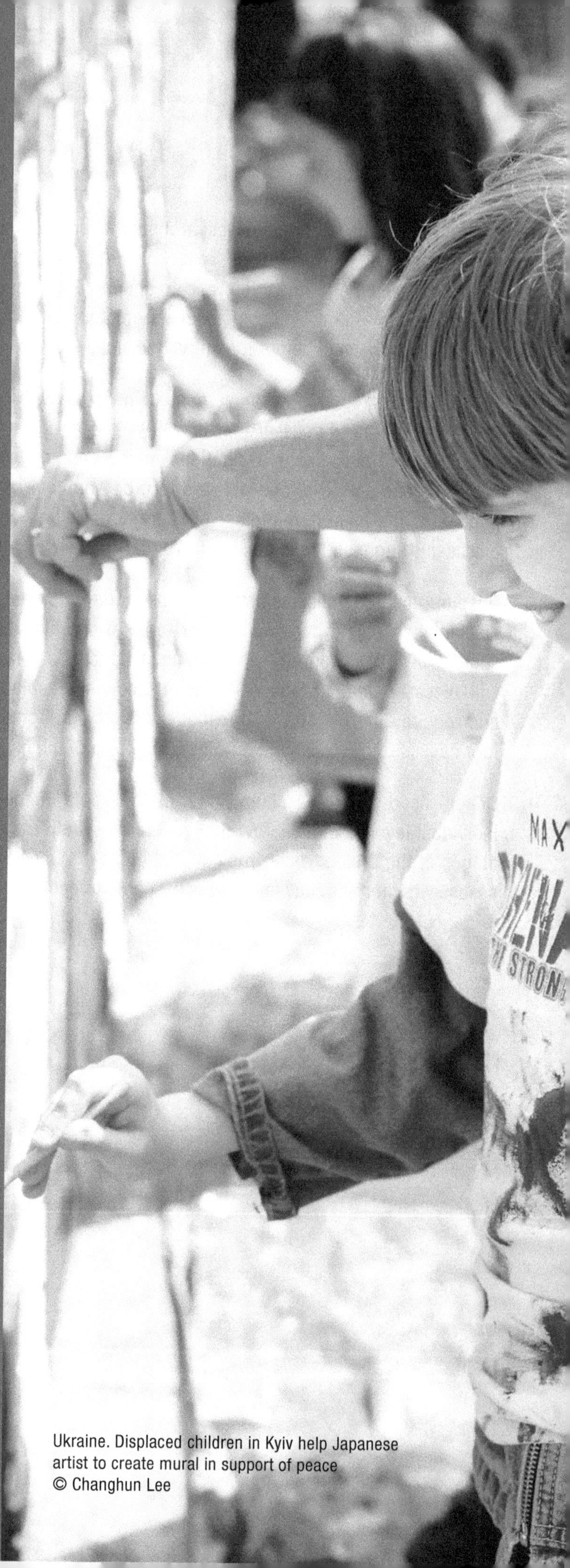

Ukraine. Displaced children in Kyiv help Japanese artist to create mural in support of peace
© Changhun Lee

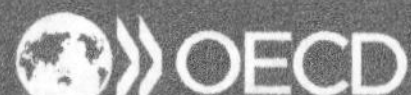

Table 3.4: Learning to learn: Effective learning strategies for donors

	Aim	Suggested Actions
Goals	• Build capabilities in operations, leadership and learning on situations of forced displacement • Improve staff opportunities for learning, e.g. through learning grants, distance learning, training courses • Improve linkages between research, evaluation and operational functions • Improve data platforms • Clarify roles and expectations for organisational and individual learning	• Develop learning plans at department and country levels • Develop an integrated approach to organisational and individual learning • Ensure that country evaluations look at forced displacement as a cross-cutting issue and that sectoral evaluations include refugees and IDPs by specifying this requirement in the terms of reference for the evaluations • Invest in maintaining institutional knowledge, e.g. through mentoring and handovers which are particularly important in dynamic contexts with high staff turnover • Provide opportunities to discuss failure in an open and constructive manner • Ensure staff are aware of organisational learning strategies and individual learning opportunities • Incentivise staff to acquire field experience, e.g. through secondments and compulsory rotation • Hold line managers to account for ensuring that learning takes place
Collections and Delivery	• Inform the development and delivery of sustainable and quality programmes • Ensure transparency and accountability to affected populations • Build, maintain and prioritise relationships with partners • Mitigate contextual risks, e.g. insecurity	• Target research and ensure it is in line with key priorities • Invest specific resources to synthesise evidence into practical, easy-to-use resources, e.g. help desks and regional resource centres • Ask affected communities about their communication preferences to facilitate regular information exchange • Use third party monitoring where access is constrained • Combine technology, e.g. digital data and big data, with more traditional approaches to monitoring and evaluation • Assess the impact of evaluations by monitoring actions taken in response to individual evaluations and their impact on overall value for money and effectiveness.
Learning	• Integrate learning into the life cycle of donor work	• Include a section on learning in mid-year and annual project reviews • Invest in continuous monitoring and provide for flexibility to adjust programmes in real time • Engage donor staff in project oversight to allow for quick learning, feedback and action • Give all staff, in particular local staff, the opportunity to contribute their knowledge • Extract insights from learning and knowledge collected by partners and contractors • Integrate feedback from affected populations into monitoring activities

Principle 3: Strengthening partnerships

A wide range of organisations and groups play different roles in responding to forced displacement, creating a complicated web of co-ordination roles and responsibilities, and partnership opportunities. Partners may be influenced by their organisational mandates or their technical expertise, or by the control of states over particular actors. Each party brings unique value to a response, as well as its own limitations. Donors should emphasise respect for the organisational mandates of specific actors, understand how different components of a response system work with each other, and strive to identify existing efficiencies as well as bottlenecks that may need to be addressed.

Donors should pursue a whole-of-government approach in hosting countries, many of which often reflect the bifurcation between development and humanitarian assistance that is characteristic of the international aid architecture. While line ministries manage public services at the national level, in some countries specific entities have been created to co-ordinate responses to forced displacement. Conflicting goals across these different parts of government can lead to stalled decision making.

Depending on the location of displaced populations, local authorities may be responsible for service provision. In certain settings, traditional leaders are also key actors in a displacement response. They may, for example, make decisions about allocation of land for settlements or access to natural resources. **Donors should not neglect the particularities of local political legitimacy, particularly in conflict-affected and fragile societies.** In Somalia, for example, political legitimacy is largely derived from the clan and religious constituencies. In South Sudan, it is based as much on war-veteran status and personal charisma as it is on ethnicity (Van Veen and Dudouet, 2017).

Identifying the right partners encourages community acceptance and contributes to an effective response. Political leadership sets tone and policy, and helps manages bilateral relations with donors. These complexities must be understood by donors seeking to invest in effective national partnerships. Donors, particularly in countries where they provide budgetary support, and where aid remains a substantial part of the budget, are in a unique position to **influence policy matters and institutional frameworks** to support coherent national development and humanitarian responses to forced displacement.

Local non-governmental organisations (NGOs) also implement programmes funded by international organisations, donors, governments, or private sources. They have differing levels of capabilities and variable presence in co-ordination structures. While their programmes can be less expensive than those of international NGOs, local NGOs may lack capacity and may experience difficulty absorbing funding from donors and United Nations (UN) agencies, as language barriers and lack of experience serve as impediments to gaining larger roles. Faith-based NGOs often provide public services and may benefit from being well-trusted by displaced populations. Donors have immense convening power to help **stimulate civil society and private sector partnerships** and can also help ensure that these efforts are aligned with donor and national policies.

In order to strengthen partnerships, donors should encourage development and humanitarian partners to **prioritise engagement with displaced communities, invest in capacity building of all key stakeholders and engage in partnerships based on a clear understanding of strategic value.** Donors should also assess opportunities for working with new partners and for linking responses at different layers of societies and institutional mechanisms.

 # 7. People-centred and community-driven programming

The World Humanitarian Summit highlighted the importance of supporting and strengthening local actors and reorienting the aid system toward a more localised approach that facilitates community-level relief and recovery efforts. This includes giving local actors a greater voice and opportunity to influence international aid policies and practices that affect their communities and larger societies.

Although policy decisions for forcibly displaced populations are usually adopted at the national level, local authorities are usually most directly affected by displacement. Local actors are often the "first responders" in a crisis and provide critical points of contact for development and humanitarian actors. Support to **multi-stakeholder forums** can bring together national and local stakeholders to discuss aid delivery, programming and effectiveness and encourage lesson learning. Donors should support local problem solving and the design of interventions that are anchored in, and compatible with, existing cultural norms and socio-political realities. **Local dynamics should be viewed as part of the context, not as part of the problem.** Programmes should be locally defined and relevant and build on, rather than undermine, domestic institutions.

> Many refugee responses are geared towards responding to refugee movements and only subsequently build in a component for host community support. Turn this model around. Encourage programmes that create an enabling host environment from the outset.

Local grassroots organisations with a presence in the community are trusted by the communities they serve and can provide insights into country contexts. Donors can also learn from local government and local CSOs and invest in building their long-term capacities. A locally-led response has the advantage of **better access and deeper networks** with affected people, a better understanding of the history and cultural and geopolitical specificities of the area and – as local actors are often themselves affected – a personal understanding of what needs to be done and the motivation to do it.

In the Middle East and North Africa (MENA) region, for example, 86% of refugees live in cities. This situation forced local authorities, who had little experience in managing large-scale refugee influxes, to adapt their functions and assume key roles by providing basic services and integrating refugees into communities. While the strain on local municipal service provision may have exacerbated tensions between host and refugee communities, and local actors had no experience of delivering a large-scale response, in many cases the influx provided an opportunity for host communities to improve infrastructure and services and to enhance their resilience (World Bank Group, 2016). In this example, responding through local municipalities influxes proved to be far more effective than providing resources to national authorities.

While most planning analysis focuses on the role of formal institutions, it is also important to understand how **informal social, political and cultural norms** shape human interaction and political competition. Map all key stakeholders and their relationships to determine what interventions may or may not work as might be the case, for example, where donor interests do not align with cultural norms.

If donors are to successfully build on, develop and help sustain local capacity, they will need to understand better where gaps in local capacity exist, to target suitable support in those areas, and gradually nurture local organisations to take greater leadership of the interventions that they support (Rabinowitz, 2013). **Acknowledging complexity means recognising that change is often best led by people who are close to the problem** and have the greatest stake in its solution, whether central or local government officials, civil society groups, private-sector groups or affected communities.

Box 3.7: Community-based responses

Agriculture and livestock support for Syria's conflict-affected populations

Coordinated by Italy and implemented by the Mediterranean Agronomic Institute of Bari in Syria, this project aims to increase the capacity of Syrian Interim Government's Ministry of Infrastructure, Agriculture and Water Resources and of the Local Council Administrations (LCAs) to provide services to the rural communities held by the moderate opposition. It also aims to increase agricultural and livestock production and household income of local communities, particularly in Syrian rural communities living in areas held by the moderate opposition.

The programme is implemented with the collaboration of LCAs, women's Associations and Syrian technicians. By 2017, thanks to this programme 11 600 farmers and breeders benefited from agricultural inputs and services including distribution of fertilizers, fodder, barley seeds; vaccinations; animal treatments; and crops diseases treatments. The programme adopts a market-based approach that is unique inside Syria, where humanitarian distribution of handouts is the norm. All inputs and services are provided to the direct beneficiaries using a "revolving fund system". This means that each beneficiary who receives services or inputs from the programme will repay them at a subsidised price that corresponds to the 75% of its value. The collected payments are then deposited in a dedicated bank account, and used to fund similar inputs and services for new beneficiaries. Up to date, the revolving fund has collected USD 1 050 595. The adoption of the revolving fund in a war-torn country has proved to be effective and sustainable, challenging the more common approach of distributing free inputs typical of humanitarian relief. The subsidised price of inputs helps lower production costs and increases the overall profitability of farmers and breeders.

8. Build capacity

Capacity building efforts should start with enhancing donors' own capacities to engage effectively in situations of forced displacement. Donors can establish **mixed humanitarian and development teams** at headquarters level or joint humanitarian-development "task forces" to respond to specific emergencies. They can also ensure consistent engagement between humanitarian and development planning at headquarter and country level, for example, by **involving country embassies** in the development of programmes instead of centralising this function at headquarters level.

Development actors **must be present and active** in situations of forced displacement if they are to contribute to effective and co-ordinated responses. Enhanced donor presence and professional expertise at field level can facilitate more systematic engagement with development and humanitarian partners. An evaluation of ECHO's response to the Syria crisis explains how ECHO's strong and early field presence enabled it to provide partners with informed support, advice, and a greater capacity to adapt to the evolving context inside Syria and neighbouring countries (ADE and URD, 2016).

Where the situation is volatile and may change rapidly between a humanitarian and development setting, it is important to maintain a certain level of **flexibility in staffing**, to ensure that they have adequate expertise and knowledge to respond to changing circumstances. In times of crisis, when decisions need to be quick and evidence-based, donors should empower staff who are most aware of the context and closest to operations. This can enhance co-ordination and timeliness of response much more than relying on short-term surge capacity.

At the multilateral level, donors should **build the capacity of senior leadership** to promote better co-ordination between humanitarian and development actors. Funding development positions in humanitarian organisations, and vice versa, can contribute to multilateral coherence. **Standby and partnership arrangements** can provide technical expertise to multilateral and national partners as needed.

State institutions have the mandate to co-ordinate and regulate responses to forced displacement. Where state or local capacity to implement does not exist, donors should **open up space for local leadership** in development processes by including state actors in the design of development and humanitarian programmes for forcibly displaced populations – where this is determined to be appropriate. Donors should integrate systematic assessments of the **impact of capacity building activities** like institutional support and technical co-operation programmes into their programming. Donors can also support the **capacity for emergency management of local responders** in partner countries. Civil protection actors in donor countries have the capacity to undertake this work. Donors can build on the experience of DAC members including Australia, Finland, Italy, Japan and New Zealand in this area (Scott, 2015).

Fiscal decentralisation and resilience building for Iraqi authorities

Funded by Canada and implemented by the Institute on Governance in Iraq between April 2015 and September 2018. It draws on lessons learnt in situations of protracted crises, which indicate that there is a need for more than the provision of basic services. Resilience must include political reform and institutional capacity building if it is to prove sustainable.

The project aims to build the capacity of local Iraqi authorities to deliver basic services to their populations, including those displaced by conflict, and to build more accountable, inclusive and effective governance in Iraq. The project is expected to reach approximately 1300 senior representatives from the political sphere, academia and officials at the federal, regional and governorate levels through their participation in networking, seminars, workshops and the building of institutional capacity.

Decentralisation can create a more robust authority structures and, at the local level, fiscal decentralisation can effectively strengthen taxation systems and increase public accountability. Strong partnerships with local authorities, particularly municipalities, who are at the front-line in meeting the challenges of the refugee crisis increases capacities to develop locally led and owned priorities and plans. Recipient authorities are often willing to listen to, and apply external advice, even in the midst of a crisis if it is provided in a way that is tailored to needs and circumstances on the ground.

Iraq. Returning families rebuild their homes in Ramadi.
© UNHCR/Caroline Gluck

OECD

9. Value-driven partnerships

Donors should prioritise partnerships that provide **value-for-money** in terms of finding a balance between economy, efficiency and effectiveness.[11] Donors should assess both the benefits and potential risks of working with specific partners, but should also consider how their overall partnership strategy can contribute to better results. For some donors, working through a limited range of partners may enhance the capacity of the donor to engage meaningfully and contribute to effectiveness. Other donors prefer to work with traditional partners, because it seems less risky, while ignoring new or unknown partners who may be more effective and efficient in specific operational contexts.

Multiple evaluations have noted the **impact of partnership arrangements** on programming outcomes. An evaluation of Australia's response to the Syria crisis found that funding was spread across too many partners, reducing its potential effectiveness. Danida meanwhile, which engaged with a smaller number of organisations, enabled it to "be a partner, not simply a donor" allowing for more flexibility in response (Ruaudel and Morrison-Métois, 2017).

Value-for-money in partnerships is about getting the right balance between three things – economy, efficiency and effectiveness. It cannot be assessed by looking at only one of these dimensions in isolation. Implementing a programme on sexual and gender-based violence (SGBV) with a newly-established local NGO may be cheaper (economy) but limited NGO capacity, due to high staff turnover due to low salary-scales, limited awareness of principles of protection, and access constraints due to perceived ethnic biases, can lead to increased protection risks (effectiveness) for women-at-risk and indicates poor value-for-money. Conversely, implementing an SGBV programme with a newly-established NGO may be cheaper and more effective, where the NGO has good awareness of protection principles, is embedded in the community and perhaps employs survivors of SGBV as peer counsellors, increasing access to beneficiaries, de-stigmatising SGBV and providing livelihoods opportunities for survivors and their families.

Particularly at the onset of a displacement crisis, donors should consider **local dynamics and systemic weaknesses** when deciding on partnerships. Where the host state is a party to conflict, or there is poor infrastructure or limited technical capacity, it may not be possible or appropriate to work through state or local authorities. Donors should also recognise that the right balance between types of aid delivery may be **context-dependent**. Countries with weak public institutional capacity may benefit from project aid, while those with strong operational programmes, solid financial management systems and evaluation mechanisms for their own development expenditures may benefit from sectoral budget support.

Working with multilateral agencies or international NGOs may be more effective at the onset of a crisis as they can mobilise international expertise, institutional capacity, and additional funding quickly in a crisis and take on roles in service provision that host governments may have difficulty performing. Donors should work with UN agencies and international NGOs to ensure these organisations build the capacity of national and local actors to carry on the long-term response. The International Federation of Red Cross and Red Crescent Societies and the International Committee of the Red Cross provide good models of collaboration with national Red Cross and Red Crescent branches.

Private sector and other non-state providers (e.g. NGOs and faith-based organisations) are often significant providers in situations of conflict and fragility. They can be more resilient than state structures, enjoy greater acceptance and proximity to needs on the ground, and be less expensive to work with. However, their performance is largely unregulated and can be uneven. Donors should consider financial management, monitoring and absorption capacity and allocate funding, directly or indirectly as appropriate, to build their capacity.

Principle 4: Delivering the right finance

In 2016, global humanitarian assistance increased for the fourth year running, reaching a new high of USD 27.3 billion. The 6% rise from 2015 was significantly lower than increases in recent years, despite the growing number of persons in need of assistance identified by UN appeals, which experienced a 40% global shortfall in funds (Development Initiatives, 2017). While DAC donors' aid spending on the cost of hosting refugees within their own borders has dramatically increased in recent years – from USD 3 billion in 2012 to USD 15.4 billion in 2016 – their humanitarian aid spending is growing at a slower pace, and amounted to USD 14.4 billion in 2016. For the first time, DAC donors are spending more on in-donor refugee costs than on humanitarian aid (OECD, 2017a).

Figure 3.2: 2015 Humanitarian Aid as a percentage of official development assistance (ODA)

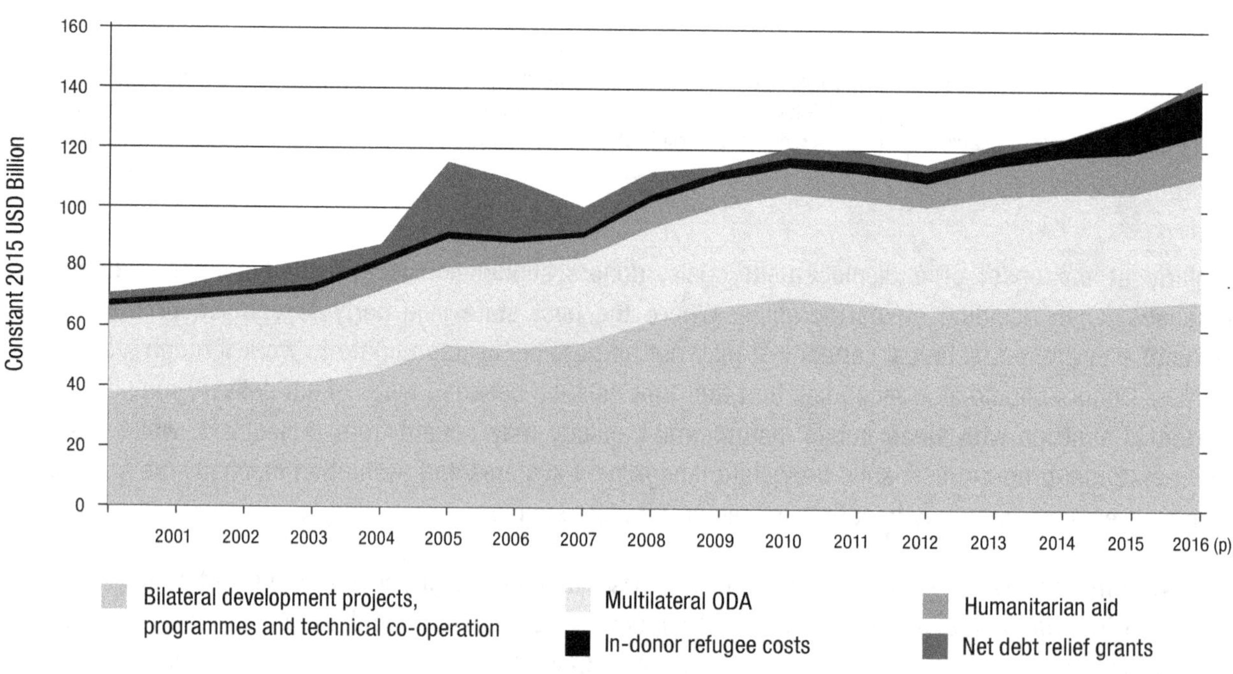

Source: OECD (2017a), *"Development aid rises again in 2016"*,
https://www.oecd.org/dac/financing-sustainable-development/development-finance-data/ODA-2016-detailed-summary.pdf.

Estimating the costs of achieving long term sustainable development globally is complex and there is no clear answer. The Sustainable Development Solutions Network estimates that low and lower-middle-income countries may need USD 1.4 trillion annually to achieve the 17 Sustainable Development Goals (SDGs) by 2030

(SDSN, 2015). The OECD meanwhile, estimates that investment needs for the SDGs in developing countries are estimated to be in the order of USD 3.3 to 4.5 trillion per year (OECD, 2016b).

> The international community should not expect situations to improve rapidly to the extent that they do not appropriately prioritise displaced populations' immediate needs for humanitarian assistance

Financing for humanitarian responses will remain essential, particularly to save lives in emergencies. Ruaudel and Morrison-Métois, 2017). Donors are encouraged to **complement additional funding for humanitarian assistance with development finance** to ensure that refugees as well as local populations have access to public services, infrastructure and economic opportunities. Donors are also encouraged to protect humanitarian budgets for emergencies by scaling up catastrophe insurance for countries and households to facilitate better disaster preparedness.

Multilateral development banks are increasingly prominent providers of crisis-related financing. In Jordan and Lebanon, the World Bank prioritised budget support to mitigate the impact of the refugee crisis on country systems and host communities. However, there are concerns that a loan approach, particularly in middle-income countries, further exacerbates the already high-level of debt (IEG, 2016). Blended financing, used largely to date in environment programming, is also an effective tool for financing in forced displacement crisis-situations. In recent years, tens of billions have been spent to stimulate investment and provide jobs at origin to address "root causes" of secondary migration. Yet some analysts have pointed out that such investments are not based on a strong understanding of the lives of refugees (Mallett, 2017). More analysis of the benefits and impact of this approach is required.

As humanitarian funding fails to keep pace and shortfalls persist, the potential of private sources of funding continues to draw attention, although funding from private donors only increased by an estimated 6% in 2016. Displaced populations are not viewed as strong potential clients by the private sector. Donor advocacy should address financial providers' misconception that refugees and IDPs are a flight risk. Donors may also need to work more intensively with private investors, local co-operatives and trade unions and do what they can to make it easier for them to do their business – including by sharing, rather than removing, risk (Anderson and Johnson, 2017)

Traditional donors should engage more consistently with so-called "new" donors. They should aim to convey good donor standards and experience to emerging donor institutions, for instance, through the OECD DAC, which encourages all providers of development co-operation to report their aid flows. More detailed information on these flows allows providers and recipients alike to make informed decisions on aid allocations and helps to identify countries and sectors that may be over- or under-funded.

Finally, donors also need to go – more systematically – beyond their funding role in protracted crises, and focus on other areas where they can add value: for example by facilitating remittance flows, which are known to play a key role in promoting sustainable solutions. They should also support efforts to halt illicit financial flows, to stem the outflow of funds from fragile and conflict-affected states, which could otherwise support development and reconstruction in countries of asylum and origin (OECD, 2014).

There is growing evidence that greater funding predictability and flexibility enables more cost-effective management of resources and improved programming outcomes in humanitarian crises. The World Food Programme (WFP) notes that multi-year funding would reduce operational costs by about 30% through reduced procurement costs. However, many donors' humanitarian funds are available on an annual basis or for an even shorter duration of six to nine months (NORAD, 2015). Many DAC members work with **annual public expenditure cycles**, making it difficult to provide long-term funding. Others prefer short-term funding because it is faster and more risk-tolerant than development instruments (Danida, 2015).

Donors should allocate multi-year un-earmarked funding, that is over two years or more, to enhance predictability and support more efficient responses. Allocations could come in the form of **multi-year funding options** (e.g. European Union and Department for International Development); **multi-year commitments** with yearly grant renewal (e.g. Danida); or **strategic partnerships agreements** instead of project grants (e.g. Danida and DFID) (Mosel and Levine, 2014). **Long-term framework agreements**, such as those piloted by the Swedish International Development Co-operation Agency (Sida), would allow partners to plan on a multi-annual basis even though they receive funding annually (Mowjee et al., 2015). Encouragingly, 16 OECD DAC members already provide multi-annual funding to select UN, NGO and Red Cross Movement partners (Scott, 2015).

Early indications suggest that returns on multi-annual investments have been uneven. Current **financial tracking platforms and standards need to be updated** to allow funding provided as part of multi-annual commitments to be identified as such, making it possible to accurately determine the scale at the global level. There is also clear scope for more co-ordination and joint action to look into the **efficiency and effectiveness of sub-contracting and related transactional costs** (Taylor et al., 2015)

Donors should support recipients of multi-year multilateral ODA and those agencies engaged in strategic flexible partnership agreements to **collect evidence to demonstrate the added value** of flexible multi-annual contributions. In this way, they can continue to build the case for a substantial increase in unearmarked contributions to multilateral humanitarian organisations. An objective study of the extent, costs and benefits of current humanitarian **sub-contracting and pass-through** funding practices should be the first step in a process to identify ways to reduce transaction costs.

Mobilising funding and bridging liquidity gaps in the early stages of crises remain major challenges. There are opportunities, however, for donors to draw on the technical expertise and analysis from private sector actors and governments to **develop objective and politically acceptable "triggers"** for the early release of funding. Making provisions for flexibility in budget management, e.g. mobilising special instruments or by facilitating the shifting of funds from other domestic policy areas and underspent funds to areas of needs – can enable responses to unforeseen crises and events.

Providing **lightly earmarked or un-earmarked funds** for programmes can also contribute to flexibility and facilitate a focus on the greatest needs. **Pooling resources** or setting aside a specific share of humanitarian and development aid for recovery can also add flexibility to existing funding pools (Steets et al., 2011).

However, pooled funding mechanisms come in various forms with different advantages and challenges. Greater information sharing and learning across the various pooled funds would encourage improvements and reduce duplication of efforts. Embedding Grand Bargain Commitments (for example, harmonised and simplified reporting, harmonised partnership agreements and assessments) in pooled funds can also contribute to improving the efficiency and effectiveness of these funds. There is an imperative to ensure these funds are as efficient as possible and that they are built to complement other funding, so that they can address the greatest humanitarian needs (Thomas, 2017). Meanwhile, in a conflict context, funding gaps can be further addressed through the expansion of peacebuilding funds and budgets, the establishment of an early recovery financing task force, and in-country piloting of early recovery funds (Chandran, et al., 2008).

At a minimum, donors need to ensure consistent communication and co-ordination both at the strategic and operational level, on their funding commitments, with other donors, government counterparts and across the humanitarian-development spectrum of implementers, to ensure all the priority aspects of a response are covered (Fabre,2017b). Donors also need to invest in more evaluations to determine the effectiveness of financing mechanisms. There is currently a general lack of evidence upon which to base funding decisions as well as limited awareness of whether the balance of funding between different delivery channels is right or wrong (Ruaudel and Morrison-Métois, 2017).

11. Better alignment

Alignment is specified in the 2005 Paris Declaration as one of five key principles of aid effectiveness. Donor funding should align with national, sub-national, and local development plans. While donors have made commitments to fund and work through national systems, definitions of "local and national partners" and of "as direct as possible" funding remain unclear.[12] The international humanitarian system was built by and for international actors, multilateral organisations and international NGOs. The complexity of modern crises calls for a review of this approach (Fabre, 2017a).

The Grand Bargain set a target of providing 25% of humanitarian funding to local and national responders "as directly as possible" to be achieved by 2020. National governmental disaster management agencies and other relevant ministries, local humanitarian responders, NGOs, and Red Cross or Red Crescent societies should be key pillars of development and humanitarian responses. Donors should address existing legal or technical barriers to funding national and local responders. While it is unquestionably important to work towards aligning development co-operation with partners' strategies, the focus should not be on funding alone. Donors should also support the development of robust systems for financial reporting, disbursement, procurement, audit, monitoring and evaluation.

Box 3.10: Investing in national systems

Access to Primary Health Care (ASSP) in the Democratic Republic of Congo

Funded by the United Kingdom, and implemented by a consortium led by IMA World Health in the DRC, the project which runs from 2013 to 2018 aims to strengthen priority health interventions that are delivered through the national health system. The ASSP currently supports 52 health zones (out of 516 nationally) in 5 of the 26 provinces in the DRC. It provides an estimated nine million people with access to essential primary and (to a lesser extent) secondary healthcare services. The programme complies with the National Health Development Plan 2016-2020 and addresses national priorities with a focus on reproductive health. The programme works closely with and supports existing healthcare structures through local delivery partners, and has enabled programme activities to continue in Kasai Central and Kasai province despite the violence and insecurity affecting these areas. The programme also works with humanitarian actors to co-ordinate the health response in the region.

It targets several different levels of intervention, including community, health facility, health zone, provincial and central levels. Activities include water, sanitation and hygiene (WASH) interventions, nutrition packages for the prevention and treatment of malnutrition, construction and renovation of health centres, provision of essential equipment, drugs/ supplies and training. The ASSP strengthens government capacity to manage health zones by enabling management teams to supervise health facilities, supports the role of provincial health divisions in management of primary health care, and provides technical assistance to the Ministry of Health to improve public financial management. It also supports the Ministry to develop and disseminate norms and standards, and has facilitated policy dialogue with faith-based providers of health services.

The country-based financing model is often challenged when responding to the needs of people living outside of their country, as in the case of refugees. Host countries may be reluctant to borrow on non-concessional terms or to use their limited allocation from the International Development Association (IDA) to address the needs of non-nationals. However, IDA-18 has a sub-window dedicated to providing resources for communities facing stress from hosting refugees that should mitigate this concern.

To secure sound public finances, **concessional lending** for part of the financing may be needed, and the availability of grants for blending may be a crucial factor. Donor should consider inserting crisis modifiers in grants to local development partners, which allows the flexibility to shift from development activities to emergency response in case of a sudden crisis (Fabre, 2017a).

With refugee and IDP finance, there is potential to exacerbate conflict or tensions between host and displaced communities and within members of displaced communities. Linked to the principle of "do no harm", development actors must avoid targeting specific market segments solely based on ethnicity, livelihood or even displacement experience, and should strive to engage host communities.

Donors should invest in the development of basic **open-source technology platforms** that can provide simple and easy access to information on the impact of aid and increase national or local ownership. In countries with limited state capacity, donors should work through local technology providers and improve their capacity to work with aid specialists (for example Twaweza in Tanzania, Ushahidi in Kenya).

There could be significant gains from **system-wide learning exercises** on alignment conducted by an independent group that includes key humanitarian stakeholders, as well as independent experts from the private sector and experts in public sector and institutional reform. Reviews should focus on the cost efficiency of practices, systems and approaches to working with national and local actors. An objective audit could help to identify existing good practices and potential cost savings.

 ## 12. More accountability

The report of the High-Level Panel on Humanitarian Financing in 2016 stressed the need for more transparent humanitarian financing, allowing all actors to **"follow the money"** from donor to recipient. Current reporting practices emphasise what goes into the system and the initial transaction between donor and the first recipient of funding. The main platforms for reporting international humanitarian and development assistance – the Financial Tracking Service of the UN Office for the Coordination of Humanitarian Affairs (OCHA) and the OECD DAC's Creditor Reporting System – are not compatible and do not effectively track the complex and lengthy transaction chains funding goes through before reaching crisis-affected populations.

> Knowing how much funding is provided to – and received by – affected populations is a prerequisite for prioritising reforms in development and humanitarian financing.

In forced displacement situations – characterised by the presence of many donors, implementers, and recipients, and few centralized ways to aggregate activities – tracking funding is particularly complex. Donors express frustration that governments cannot report how much money they have received from various sources, while governments are unhappy that they lack a complete picture of how aid funds from around the world are being spent in their countries (Culbertson et al., 2016).

The **Country Programme Aid** (CPA) measure can go some way to addressing host government concerns regarding transparency in development financing. The CPA reflects the amount of aid subject to multi-year planning at country and regional level and is defined through the exclusion of assistance that is unpredictable by nature, entails no cross-border flows, does not form part of co-operation agreements between governments, and is not country programmable by the donor. However, the measure is not perfect. CPA measures aid from the donors' perspective: still included is technical co-operation, which in many cases does not follow recipients' procedures. Likewise, the CPA allows for project-specific donor contracts with NGOs: which are not generally subjected to host government scrutiny. In fragile states there may be a case for adapting the CPA definition to include humanitarian assistance, given that this represents a large part of the total aid package to these countries for long periods. Finally, further work is required to improve the comparability of bilateral and multilateral shares of the CPA (Benn et al., 2010).

Incentives for aid transparency and accountability may vary significantly within recipient governments. While it may not be possible to institute accountability practices across the board, donors could identify potential **accountability "champions"** within governments to provide leadership and establish good practice parameters. Accountability can also be encouraged by building a shared vision of success with government partners (e.g. by agreeing jointly on targets), rewarding good practice and publicising accomplishments. Donors should focus on both **upward and downward accountability**, with a focus on building chains of accountability between service providers, governments and affected populations.

Donors should make efforts to improve information sharing on humanitarian and development funding streams. **Knowing who is receiving what funding for what purpose** will facilitate better linkages and complementary responses. Donor country personnel should also have a clear awareness of both in-country humanitarian and development activities and should systematically engage in relevant co-ordination platforms across both sectors.

Traditional donors should also reach out to new donors and engage them in accountability processes while being realistic about the timeframes for implementation. A first step may include scoping the availability of information and data from new donors and highlighting existing gaps at the country level. It is important to note that twenty non-DAC emerging donors already report in the OECD's Common Reporting Standard.[13] The OECD and DAC members are also working to modernise development finance statistics through an inclusive process, to promote uniform reporting that is credible and relevant, capturing new and more complex financing instruments and arrangements, and creating appropriate incentives for resource mobilisation. A new proposed measure of Total Official Support for Sustainable Development (TOSSD) may further contribute to the transparency of public efforts to support sustainable development.

Ground Truth Solutions

Ground Truth Solutions provides donors, development actors and humanitarian agencies with direct feedback from people affected by crisis, allowing organisations to systematically integrate this vital information into relief programmes around the world. Accurate, unbiased information, collected on the ground and in real time, allows aid agencies to take better decisions and to provide the right support. UN agencies, NGOs, as well as the Red Cross movement can use this feedback as a tool to manage and shape projects as they are being rolled out and to maximise their effectiveness. Donors can use the information to track how and where their support is making a difference. Those in need of assistance and protection are better served, where their views are fully taken into account.

For example, Ground Truth Solutions and the OECD collaborated to track first-hand how people affected by humanitarian crises – as well as humanitarian field staff who implement humanitarian programmes – perceive the reforms spelled out in the Grand Bargain document. Ground Truth Solutions developed three survey instruments to measure both the implementation and the effects of these reforms. The first set of surveys gathers feedback from affected people on the provision of humanitarian aid and track how perceptions evolve over time. The second survey instrument collects feedback from frontline staff on how Grand Bargain themes are being carried out and provides a baseline to track their progress and impact. The third survey instrument looks at relations among international agencies and local partners in the context of empowering the latter to play a larger role in humanitarian relief operations.

Throughout history, communities living next to crisis zones, as well as those far from the frontlines, have welcomed the uprooted and given them shelter – and in return, refugees have given back. Today 84 percent of the world's refugees are hosted by low- or middle-income countries. We cannot continue to allow a small number of countries – often the world's poorest – to shoulder this weight alone. This not about sharing a burden. It is about sharing a global responsibility, based not only the broad idea of our common humanity but also on the very specific obligations of international law.

Antonio Guterres, UN Secretary General, Statement on World Refugee Day, June 20, 2017

Principle 1: Increasing understanding

Inter-Agency Standing Committee (IASC) Task Team on Humanitarian and Development Nexus, co-chaired by UNDP and WHO, developed a toolkit to support planning across humanitarian, peace and development fields.

Internal Displacement Monitoring Centre (IDMC) is a valuable source of comprehensive statistics on conflict and disaster-induced IDPs.

Internal Organization for Migration (IOM) Global Migration Data Analysis Centre provides key information about global migration from a variety of agencies and national statistical offices.

Joint IDP Profiling Service is an inter-agency service that supports government, humanitarian and development actors to design and implement collaborative profiling exercises for IDP situations.

OECD Development Assistance and Approaches to Risk in Fragile and Conflict Affected States.

OECD Guidelines for Resilience Systems Analysis: How to Analyse Risk and Build a Roadmap for Resilience.

OECD's International Migration Outlook analyses migration flows in OECD countries and selected non-member countries and includes some information on refugees as well as a useful statistical annex.

Population Statistics Database provides UNHCR data on refugees, IDPs and stateless populations.

Putting Learning at the Centre: Adaptive Development Programming in Practice.

Refworld is a UN Refugee Agency (UNHCR) site providing access to laws, case law and country of origin information.

Principle 2: Learning through evidence

ACAPS (the Assessment Capacities Project).

ALNAP develops guidance on humanitarian evaluation, provides a repository of knowledge through the HELP library and offers a platform for evaluators to be in touch with their peers.

DAC Network on Development Evaluation Resource Centre (DEReC) is a database of DAC member evaluations.

Humanitarian Innovation Project undertakes research on refugee economies; bottom-up innovation; military-humanitarian innovation; and governance innovation.

Independent Evaluation Group evaluates the development effectiveness of the World Bank Group.

IOM evaluation provides evaluations of policies, strategies and or programmes on migration and forced displacement.

OECD Development Co-operation Report 2017: Data for Development.

REACH is an online platform that provides access to reports, factsheets, maps and other products.

Secure Access in Volatile Environments (SAVE) 2016 Toolkit of Technologies for Monitoring in Insecure Environments.

UN Evaluation Group is an interagency professional network that brings together the evaluation units of the UN system.

Principle 3: Strengthening partnerships

Cash Learning Partnership (CaLP) is a global partnership of humanitarian actors engaged in policy, practice and research within cash transfer programming (CTP).

Cisco Tactical Operations (TacOps) deploy highly secure communication networks during emergencies and foster co-operation between private and public sector organisations.

Collective Impact for the Digital Impact Alliance (DIAL) improves access to, understanding of and use of data for development in public service delivery and development programmes.

Global Programs, Humanitarian Disaster Management, NetHope enables cross-sector collaboration with non-profits to develop programmes, mitigate risks, and scale benefits in conflict-affected communities.

GSMA Mobile for Development, Disaster Response Programme advances the use of mobile technology for development and humanitarian responses.

Innovations for Poverty Action collects and disseminates evidence on effective solutions to global poverty problems to decision-makers.

Multi-Sector Initial Rapid Assessment Guidelines.

Principles of Partnership is a tool for organisations participating in the global humanitarian platform.

Real Impact Analytics bridges the gap between telecom operators and development agency end users.

Smarter Partnerships: Realising the true potential of a global partnership for development.

Vodafone's Instant Network Emergency Response deploys people and technology to provide free communication and technical support in areas affected by natural or humanitarian disasters.

Principle 4: Delivering the right finance

Consultative Group to Assist the Poor (CGAP) is a global partnership of 34 leading organisations that seek to increase access to the financial services the poor need to improve their lives.

EDRIS contains real time information on ECHO and member states' contributions to humanitarian aid.

Financial Tracking Service (FTS) is a global humanitarian financial reporting platform and service managed by OCHA under the oversight of the Inter-Agency Standing Committee (IASC).

IASC Humanitarian Financing Task Team

International Aid Transparency Initiative (IATI) is a voluntary, multi-stakeholder initiative that seeks to improve the transparency of aid, development, and humanitarian resources.

Making Finance Work for Africa

The Bill and Melinda Gates Foundation (BMGF) Financial Services for the Poor Initiatives

OECD Development Co-operation 2016: The Sustainable Development goals as Business Opportunities

Financing the UN Development System: Pathways to Reposition for Agenda 2030

UN Secretary-General's Report on the UN Development System

Notes

1 Examples of relevant actors to consider are: displaced persons and host communities, traditional and religious leaders, national and local NGOs, national and local political leadership, businesses, diaspora networks, donors, multilateral development banks, intergovernmental organisations and others.

2 While most analysis focuses on the role of formal institutions, it is also important to understand how informal social, political and cultural norms shape human interaction and political competition.

3 Effective co-ordination of humanitarian action in the field hinges upon the Humanitarian Coordinators. While the primary responsibility for coordinating humanitarian assistance rests with national authorities, if international humanitarian assistance is required the HC is responsible for leading and coordinating the efforts of humanitarian organisations (both UN and non-UN). The cluster approach was introduced to ensure that there is predictable leadership and accountability in all main sectors or areas of humanitarian response and to strengthen system-wide preparedness and technical capacity to respond to humanitarian emergencies. To this purpose, global cluster leads were designated in the following sectors: Camp Co-ordination and Camp Management, Early Recovery, Education, Food Security, Emergency Telecommunications, Health, Logistics, Nutrition, Shelter, Water, Sanitation and Hygiene, and Protection. For refugee emergencies, the Refugee Co-ordination Model applies. The Refugee Coordinator is often the UNHCR Representative in medium-sized emergencies and the Emergency Coordinator or Deputy or Assistant Representative in larger ones. The planning process for the Refugee Response Plan should be inclusive and should involve all key actors, including representatives of the host Government (where possible), members of the UN or Humanitarian Country Team, development actors, and participating responders. In more protracted situations, UNHCR is rolling out the CRRF to bridge the humanitarian – development divide. The CRRF Secretariat structure includes line ministries, regional and district authorities, in order to promote a whole-of-society approach.

4 INCAF is a subsidiary body of the OECD DAC.

5 As many responses to forced displacement occur in fragile and conflict-affected contexts, donors are also encouraged to give due consideration to current thinking on standard good practice for development support in fragile, at-risk and conflict-affected contexts. See, http://dx.doi.org/10.1787/24140929.

6 In the past donors have committed to improving common planning and communication but have failed to implement this beyond regional or thematic exchange of information. Section 2.1 of this guide provides a starting point for thinking around common challenges and actions for improved co-ordination and common planning. Consult the Table 2.2: Challenges to donor co-ordination in situations of forced displacement on page 36.

7 In South Sudan, for example, OCHA compiles statistics on IDPs using data received on an ad hoc basis from the government's South Sudan Relief and Rehabilitation Commission, UN agencies, international organisations (such as IOM), NGOs, local authorities and community leaders.

8 Refugees and IDPs are often not covered by national poverty statistics, which are usually based on household surveys that can leave such groups excluded. It is important to include forcibly displaced populations in national poverty estimates as they often have very different poverty profiles compared to host communities. These change according to the length and causes of displacement, the economic background from which they have fled, and the socio-economic circumstances of exile.

9 Some donors supported efforts to improve the quality of data, information sharing and to strengthen needs assessments, funding initiatives such as ACAPs, the Syria Needs Analysis Project (SNAP) and REACH (a joint initiative of the United Nations Operational Satellite Applications Programme and the Agency for Technical Cooperation and Development). Nevertheless, an evaluation of ECHO's response in Syria cited challenges related to the presence of multiple needs assessments with issues in regards to the compatibility and comparability of datasets and assessments.

10 Though limited to participating members, the DAC Peer Reviews, which take place about every five years, are an example of an existing mechanism for reflection that can offer a mutual learning space on development practices

11 Value-for-money is not about monetising everything and applying cost-benefit or cost-effectiveness analyses. These are tools which may be relevant to assessing value for money in some cases, but value-for-money is a much broader concept. In some contexts applying value-for-money may not relate to tools and calculations but to applying a way of thinking to designing, programming and reviewing development co-operation

12 A duplication of work between the Grand Bargain and Humanitarian Financing Task Team (HFTT) on localisation has resulted in two sets of definitions for local and national actors. For the purposes of this guidance therefore, readers are referred to the typology of local humanitarian responders developed for the OECD Commitments into Action Series on "Localising the Response," www.oecd.org/development/humanitarian-donors/docs/Localisingtheresponse.pdf

13 See www.oecd.org/development/stats/non-dac-reporting.htm

Works cited

ACAPS (2016), *Crisis Overview 2016: Humanitarian Trends and Risks for 2017*, Assessment Capacities Project, Geneva, https://www.acaps.org/special-report/crisis-overview-2016-humanitarian-trends-and-risks-2017.

ACAPS (2013), *Compared to What? Analytical thinking and needs assessment*, Assessment Capacities Project, Geneva, https://www.acaps.org/compared-what-analytical-thinking-and-needs-assessment.

ADE and URD (2016), *Evaluation of the ECHO Response to the Syria Crisis 2012-2014*, Directorate-General for European Civil Protection and Humanitarian Aid Operations, Brussels, http://ec.europa.eu/echo/sites/echo-site/files/syria_evaluation_report.pdf.

Anderson, T. and D. Johnson (2017), *Financing the Frontier: Inclusive Financial Sector Development in Fragility-Affected States in Africa*, Financial Sector Deepening Africa and Mercy Corps, Nairobi, http://www.fsdafrica.org/wp-content/uploads/2017/02/17-02-13-Mercy-Corps-Report.pdf.

Angenendt, S. and A. Koch (2017), *Global Migration Governance and Mixed Flows: Implications for Development-centred Policies*, Stiftung Wissenschaft und Politik, Berlin, https://www.swp-berlin.org/fileadmin/contents/products/research_papers/2017RP08_adt_koh.pdf.

Angenendt, S. et al. (2016b), *Many Refugees, Poor Data: Development Co-operation Requires Higher Quality Data*, Stiftung Wissenschaft und Politik, Berlin, https://www.swp-berlin.org/fileadmin/contents/products/comments/2016C37_adt_kpp_koh.pdf.

Benn, J. et al. (2010), "Getting Closer to the Core – Measuring Country Programmable Aid", Development Brief, Issue 1, OECD Publishing, Paris, https://www.oecd.org/dac/aid-architecture/45564447.pdf.

Borton, J. (2004), *The Joint Evaluation of Emergency Assistance to Rwanda*, Humanitarian Practice Network, London, http://odihpn.org/magazine/the-joint-evaluation-of-emergency-assistance-to-rwanda/.

Chandran, R. et al. (2008), *Recovering from War: Gaps in Early Action*, DFID, London, https://www.alnap.org/system/files/content/resource/files/main/cic-earlyrecoveryfinal.pdf.

Culbertson, S. et al. (2016), *Rethinking co-ordination of services to refugees in urban areas: Managing the crisis in Jordan and Lebanon*, RAND Corporation, Santa Monica, https://www.alnap.org/system/files/content/resource/files/main/rethinking-coordination-of-services-to-refugees.pdf.

Danida (2015), *Evaluation of the Strategy for Danish Humanitarian Action 2010-2015*, Ministry of Foreign Affairs of Denmark, Copenhagen, https://www.oecd.org/derec/denmark/Evaluation-strategy-Danish-humanitarian-action-2010-2015.pdf.

Development Initiatives (2016), *Global Humanitarian Assistance Report 2016*, Development Initiatives, Bristol, http://devinit.org/post/global-humanitarian-assistance-report-2016/#.

Evalnet (2010), *Development Evaluation Resources and Systems: A study of members of the OECD Network on Development Evaluation*, OECD Publishing, Paris.

Eyben, R. (2005), "Donors' Learning Difficulties: Results, Relationships and Responsibilities", *IDS Bulletin*, Vol. 36/3, Institute of Development Studies, Brighton, pp. 98-107.

Fabre, C. (2017a), "Localising the Response", *The Commitments Into Action Series*, OECD Publishing, Paris, https://www.oecd.org/development/humanitarian-donors/docs/Localisingtheresponse.pdf.

Fabre, C. (2017b), "Multi-year Humanitarian Funding", *The Commitments Into Action Series*, OECD Publishing, OECD, http://www.oecd.org/development/humanitarian-donors/docs/multiyearfunding.pdf.

IEG (2016), *World Bank Group Engagement in Situations of Fragility, Conflict and Violence*, Independent Evaluation Group, World Bank, Washington, DC, https://openknowledge.worldbank.org/handle/10986/24915.

Jansury, L. et al. (2015), *Findings in Monitoring and Evaluation Practices in Humanitarian Emergencies*, George Washington University, Washington, DC, https://elliott.gwu.edu/sites/elliott.gwu.edu/files/IBTCI.pdf.

Krystalli, R. and E. Ott (2015), *Evidence Synthesis in the Humanitarian Sector: A Humanitarian Evidence Programme Guidance Note*, Oxfam-Feinstein International Center, Somerville, http://fic.tufts.edu/assets/Humanitarian-Evidence-Program-Guidance-Note.pdf.

Mallett, R. (2017), "Journeys on hold: How policy influences the migration decisions of Eritreans in Ethiopia", *Working Paper*, No. 506, ODI, London, https://www.odi.org/sites/odi.org.uk/files/resource-documents/11336.pdf.

Mosel, I. and S. Levine (2014), *Remaking the case for linking relief, rehabilitation, and development: How LRRD can become a practically useful concept for assistance in difficult places*, Humanitarian Policy Group at the Overseas Development Institute, London, https://www.odi.org/sites/odi.org.uk/files/odi-assets/publications-opinion-files/8882.pdf.

Mowjee, T. et al. (2015), *Coherence in Conflict: Bringing humanitarian and development aid streams together*, Danida, Copenhagen, https://www.humanitarianoutcomes.org/file/77/download?token=P99VgU7j.

Norad (2015), *Striking the Balance: Evaluation of the Planning, Organisation and Management of Norwegian Assistance Related to the Syrian Regional Crisis*, Norwegian Agency for Development Cooperation, Oslo.

O'Dwyer, B. (2005), "Stakeholder democracy: challenges and contributions from social accounting", *Business Ethics: A European Review*, Vol 14/1, Wiley, Hoboken, pp. 28-41.

OECD (2017a), *Development aid rises again in 2016*, OECD Publishing, Paris, https://www.oecd.org/dac/financing-sustainable-development/development-finance-data/ODA-2016-detailed-summary.pdf.

OECD (2016b), *Development Co-operation Report 2016: The Sustainable Development Goals as Business Opportunities*, OECD Publishing, Paris, http://dx.doi.org/10.1787/dcr-2016-en.

OECD (2015), *Development Assistance and Approaches to Risk in Fragile and Conflict Affected States*, OECD Publishing, Paris.

OECD, 2014. *Guidelines for resilience systems analysis*, OECD Publishing, Paris, https://www.oecd.org/dac/Resilience%20Systems%20Analysis%20FINAL.pdf.

MacLeman, H. et al. (2016), *Resilience Systems Analysis: Learning & recommendations report*, OECD Publishing, Paris, https://www.oecd.org/dac/conflict-fragility-resilience/docs/SwedenLearning_Recommendationsreport.pdf.

PRMN (2017), *Somalia: Displacements dashboard*, Protection & Return Monitoring Network, UNHCR, Geneva, https://data2.unhcr.org/en/documents/details/58901.

Rabinowitz, G. (4 July 2013), "Localising aid to NGOs: issues and challenges highlighted by a multi-country study", *Comment*, ODI, London, https://www.odi.org/comment/7578-local-capacity-localising-aid-ngos-donors-hiv-aids.

Ruaudel, H. and S. Morrison-Métois (2017), "Responding to Refugee Crises in Developing Countries: What Can We Learn From Evaluations?", *OECD Development Co-operation Working Papers*, No. 37, OECD Publishing, Paris, http://dx.doi.org/10.1787/ae4362bd-en.

Scott, R. (2015), *Financing in Crisis? Making humanitarian finance fit for the future*, OECD Publishing, Paris, http://www.oecd.org/dac/OECD-WP-Humanitarian-Financing-Crisis%20.pdf.

SDSN (2015), *Investment Needs to Achieve the Sustainable Development Goals: Understanding the Billions and Trillions*, UN Sustainable Development Solutions Network, New York, http://unsdsn.org/resources/publications/sdg-investment-needs/.

Steets, J. et al. (2011), *Donor Strategies for Addressing the Transition Gap and Linking Humanitarian and Development Assistance*, Global Public Policy Institute, Berlin, http://www.gppi.net/fileadmin/user_upload/media/pub/2011/steets_2011_transition_web.pdf.

Taylor, G. et al. (2015), *Review of the Netherlands Humanitarian Assistance 2009-2014*, Netherlands Ministry of Foreign Affairs, The Hague, https://www.humanitarianoutcomes.org/file/67/download?token=mMdzD22n.

Thomas, M. (2017), *"Understanding Humanitarian Funds: Going beyond Country-based Pooled Funds"*, NRC, Oslo, https://www.nrc.no/globalassets/pdf/reports/pooled_funds_2017_16mar2017_web_v2.pdf.

Thomson, J. (2017), "The Role of Resettlement in Refugee Responsibility Sharing", *Global Leadership and Cooperation for Refugees Series*, Paper no. 3, CIGI, Waterloo, https://www.cigionline.org/sites/default/files/documents/Refugee%20Paper%20no.3_0.pdf.

Van Veen, E. and V. Dudouet (2017), *Hitting the target but missing the point: Assessing donor support for inclusive and legitimate politics in fragile states*, OECD, Paris, https://www.oecd.org/dac/conflict-fragility-resilience/docs/Hitting_the_target.pdf.

Vowles, P. (4 September 2016), "Finding Failure", Medium, https://medium.com/@PeteVowles/finding-failure-d0b365cc649d.

World Bank Group (2016), *Municipalities at the forefront of the Syrian refugee crisis*, World Bank, Washington, DC, http://www.worldbank.org/en/news/feature/2016/08/03/municipalities-at-the-forefront-of-the-syrian-refugee-crisis.

Zetter, R. (2012), *Guidelines for Assessing the Impacts and Costs of Forced Displacement*, World Bank, Washington, DC, http://siteresources.worldbank.org/EXTSOCIALDEVELOPMENT/Resources/244362-1265299949041/6766328-1265299960363/SME338-Impac-Report_v8.pdf.

Glossary

Accountability – Accountability of governments to domestic constituents for achieving development objectives is a core principle of the Paris Declaration on Aid Effectiveness. The Accra Agenda for Action broadens the concept to include engagement with parliament, political parties, local authorities, the media, academia, social partners and civil society organisations.

Alignment – Alignment means that donors base their support on partner countries' national development strategies, institutions and procedures. For example, donors commit to use country systems as the default option for programmes managed by the public sector. In return, developing countries improve the quality and transparency of their public financial management systems. A lack of alignment leads to unsustainable outcomes and undermines national institutions and processes.

Assisted Voluntary Returns and Reintegration (AVRR) – Programmes carried out by the International Organisation for Migration to support the return and reintegration of beneficiaries who include: individuals whose application for asylum was rejected or withdrawn; stranded migrants; victims of trafficking, and other vulnerable groups, including unaccompanied migrant children, or those with health-related needs.

Concessional loans – Loans extended on terms substantially more generous than market loans. Concessionality is achieved either through interest rates below those available on the market or by grace periods, or a combination of these. Concessional loans typically have long grace periods.

Diaspora – Populations outside their country of origin usually sustaining ties and developing links both with that country of origin and across countries of settlement or residence.

Durable solutions – A solution is achieved when a person can rely on a durable legal status to ensure the national protection of all of their rights, civil, political, economic, social and cultural.1 Refugee law and the UN Refugee Agency (UNHCR) recognise that durable solutions for refugees can be achieved through: voluntary repatriation, local integration, and resettlement to a third country, or through complementary pathways that allow refugees to safely take up opportunities for work, study and family reunion, and that ultimately offer a solution to their international protection needs. There is no hierarchy of durable solutions; rather, an integrated approach that combines all three solutions and takes into account opportunities and systematically addresses barriers. This approach should be implemented in close co-operation with countries of origin, host states, humanitarian and development actors, as well as refugees and host communities themselves.

Economy – The degree to which a production process minimises the cost of resources used for an activity, while considering quality.

Efficiency – An efficient activity maximises output for a given input, or minimises input for a given output and, in so doing, pays due regard to appropriate quality.

Effectiveness – The extent to which the development intervention's objectives were achieved, or are expected to be achieved, taking into account their relative importance.

Emergency – A humanitarian emergency is an event or series of events that represents a critical threat to the health, safety, security or wellbeing of a community or other large group of people, usually over a wide area. The priority in any emergency response is to save lives and reduce suffering by providing life-saving assistance such as shelter, food, water and health care.

Evaluation – The systematic and objective assessment of an on-going or completed project, programme or policy, its design, implementation and results. The aim is to determine the relevance and fulfilment of objectives, development efficiency, effectiveness, impact and sustainability. An evaluation should provide information that is credible and useful, enabling the incorporation of lessons learned into the decision-making process of both recipients and donors. Evaluation also refers to the process of determining the worth or significance of an activity, policy or programme. An assessment, as systematic and objective as possible, of a planned, on-going, or completed development intervention.

Evidence – Information that helps to substantiate, prove or disprove the truth of a specific proposition.

Fragility – Fragile contexts are defined as per the report by the Organisation for Economic Co-operation and Development (OECD), States of Fragility 2016, which characterises fragility as a combination of exposure to risk and a lack of coping capacity to manage, absorb or mitigate those risks.

Internally displaced persons (IDPs) – Persons or groups who have been forced to leave their home or place of habitual residence, in particular as a result of or in order to avoid the effects of armed conflict, situations of generalized violence, violations of human rights, or natural or man-made disasters, and who have not crossed an international border. They are nationals or habitual residents of the country concerned.

Information – Any data that may inform understanding or belief, presented in a context that gives the data meaning. Information may be true or false and only becomes evidence once it is linked to a specific proposition.

Innovation – A means of adaptation and improvement through finding and scaling solutions to problems, in the form of products, processes or wider business models.

Migrants – Persons who (a) are outside the territory of the State of which they are nationals or citizens and are in the territory of another State; (b) do not enjoy the general legal recognition of rights which is inherent in the granting by the host State of the status of refugee, naturalised person or of similar status; (c) do not enjoy either general legal protection of their fundamental rights by virtue of diplomatic agreements, visas or other agreements.

Migration management – Governmental functions within national systems that aim for the orderly and humane management of cross-border migration.

Non-refoulement – The protection against return to a country where a person has reason to fear persecution. Non-refoulement is the most essential component of refugee status and asylum, and is one of the basic provisions of the 1951 United Nations Convention Relating to the Status of Refugees, referenced in Article 33(1), to which no reservations are permitted, and which has been recognised as a principle of customary international law.

Protection – All activities aimed at obtaining full respect for the rights of the individual in accordance with the letter and spirit of the relevant bodies of law, namely human rights law, international humanitarian law and refugee law.

Protracted situation – A situation in which 25,000 refugees or more have been in exile "for 5 years or more after their initial displacement, without immediate prospects for implementation of durable solutions" (UNHCR ExCom, 2009). Protracted internal displacement situations are those in which "the process for finding durable solutions is stalled, and/or IDPs are marginalised as a consequence of violations or a lack of protection of human rights, including economic, social and cultural rights" (Brookings Bern Project on Internal Displacement, 2007).

Refugee – Any person who meets the eligibility criteria in the refugee definition provided by relevant international or regional refugee instruments, UNHCR's mandate, or national legislation, as appropriate. According to many of these instruments, a refugee is a person who, being outside their country of origin or habitual residence, cannot return to country of origin owing to a well-founded fear of being persecuted for reasons of race, religion, nationality, membership of a particular social group or political opinion, or, who is compelled to leave their country of origin because of indiscriminate violence or other events seriously disturbing public order, or is experiencing a threat to life, safety or freedom as a result thereof.

Resettlement – The selection and transfer of refugees from a State in which they have sought protection to a third State that has agreed to admit them – as refugees – with permanent residence status. Only a limited number of states offer resettlement on a regular basis, allocating budgets, devising programmes and providing annual resettlement quotas. Some countries also accept refugees for resettlement on an ad hoc basis but have not officially established regular resettlement programmes with annual quotas. Resettlement can also refer to the voluntary relocation of IDPs to other parts of the country as part of a durable solution.

Resilience – The ability of households, communities and nations to absorb and recover from shocks, whilst positively adapting and transforming their structures and means for living in the face of long-term stresses, change and uncertainty.

Results Based Management – A management strategy focusing on performance and achievement of outputs, outcomes and impacts.

Returnees – Former refugees or IDPs who have returned to their country or place of origin, either spontaneously or in an organized fashion, but who have yet to fully re-establish themselves in a sustainable manner and be fully integrated into the community. These returns should take place under conditions of voluntariness, safety and dignity.

Risk – The combination of the probability of an event and its negative consequences.

Self-reliance – The ability of individuals, households or communities to meet their essential needs and enjoy their social and economic rights in a sustainable manner and with dignity. Self-reliant persons lead independent and productive lives and are able to build strong social, economic and cultural ties with their host communities. Self-reliance is achieved when persons of concern are better protected by strengthening their capacity and are able to claim their civil, cultural, economic, political and social rights through the channels available to all residence of the same country, state or region, without recourse to support specific to their legal status.

Shock – A sudden event with an important and often negative impact on the vulnerability of a system and its parts. Shocks represent significant negative (or positive) impacts on people's means of living and on the functioning of a state.

Social Protection – public actions that enhance the capacity of poor people to participate in, contribute to and benefit from economic, social and political life of their communities and societies.

Stress – A long-term trend that weakens the potential of a given system and deepens the vulnerability of its actors.

System – A unit of society (for example, an individual, a household, a group of people with common characteristics, a community, or a nation), of ecology (for example, a forest) or a physical entity (for example, an urban infrastructure network).

Voluntary repatriation – The return of refugees to their country of origin. The repatriation of refugees must be voluntary, based upon a free and an informed choice. The principle of voluntariness is the cornerstone of international protection with respect to the return of refugees. Repatriation that is voluntary is far more likely to be lasting and sustainable. The requirement of voluntariness therefore constitutes a pragmatic and sensible approach towards finding a truly durable solution. "Voluntariness" implies an absence of any physical, psychological or material pressure. This is often influenced by the various types of pressure (for example, political, material and security-related) that dictate many refugees' decision to return.

Vulnerability – Susceptibility to harm and exposure to hazard.

Bibliography

ACAPS (2016), *Crisis Overview 2016: Humanitarian Trends and Risks for 2017*, Assessment Capacities Project, Geneva, https://www.acaps.org/special-report/crisis-overview-2016-humanitarian-trends-and-risks-2017.

ACAPS (2013), *Compared to What? Analytical thinking and needs assessment*, Assessment Capacities Project, Geneva, https://www.acaps.org/compared-what-analytical-thinking-and-needs-assessment.

Adam, J. (2008), "Displacement, Coping Mechanisms and the Emergence of New Markets in Ambon", *CRG Working Papers*, No. 2008/09, Conflict Research Group, Ghent, http://citeseerx.ist.psu.edu/viewdoc/download?doi=10.1.1.488.4588&rep=rep1&type=pdf.

ADE and URD (2016), *Evaluation of the ECHO Response to the Syria Crisis 2012-2014*, Directorate-General for European Civil Protection and Humanitarian Aid Operations, Brussels, http://ec.europa.eu/echo/sites/echo-site/files/syria_evaluation_report.pdf.

ALNAP (2015), *The State of the Humanitarian System*, Active Learning Network for Accountability and Performance in Humanitarian Action, London, http://sohs.alnap.org/#introduction.

Anderson, T. and D. Johnson (2017), *Financing the Frontier: Inclusive Financial Sector Development in Fragility-Affected States in Africa*, Financial Sector Deepening Africa and Mercy Corps, Nairobi, http://www.fsdafrica.org/wp-content/uploads/2017/02/17-02-13-Mercy-Corps-Report.pdf.

Angenendt, S. and A. Koch (2017), *Global Migration Governance and Mixed Flows: Implications for Development-centred Policies*, Stiftung Wissenschaft und Politik, Berlin, https://www.swp-berlin.org/fileadmin/contents/products/research_papers/2017RP08_adt_koh.pdf.

Angenendt, S. et al. (2017), *More Coherence! External Dimensions of a Comprehensive Migration and Refugee Policy – Insights from Germany*, Migration Strategy Group, Berlin, http://www.gmfus.org/publications/more-coherence-external-dimensions-comprehensive-migration-and-refugee-policy-%E2%80%94.

Angenendt, S. et al. (2016a), "Development co-operation and addressing root causes", *Forced Migration Review*, Vol. 52, Refugee Studies Centre, Oxford, pp. 29-30.

Angenendt, S. et al. (2016b), *Many Refugees, Poor Data: Development Co-operation Requires Higher Quality Data*, Stiftung Wissenschaft und Politik, Berlin, https://www.swp-berlin.org/fileadmin/contents/products/comments/2016C37_adt_kpp_koh.pdf.

Aolain, F. N. (2011), "Women, Vulnerability and Humanitarian Emergencies", *Michigan Journal of Gender and Law*, Vol. 18/1, University of Michigan Law School, Ann Arbor, pp. 1-22.

Benn, J. et al. (2010), "Getting Closer to the Core – Measuring Country Programmable Aid", *Development Brief*, Issue 1, OECD Publishing, Paris, https://www.oecd.org/dac/aid-architecture/45564447.pdf.

Bennett, C. (April 2016), "Time to Let Go: A Three-Point Proposal to Change the Humanitarian System", *ODI video*, https://www.odi.org/opinion/10346-video-three-point-proposal-change-humanitarian-system.

Bennett, C. (2015), "The development agency of the future: Fit for protracted crises?", *Working Paper*, ODI, London, https://www.odi.org/sites/odi.org.uk/files/odi-assets/publications-opinion-files/9612.pdf.

Betz, F. and G. Frewer (2016), *Neighbourhood SME financing: Jordan*, European Investment Bank, Luxembourg, http://www.eib.org/attachments/efs/economic_report_neighbourhood_sme_financing_jordan_en.pdf.

BMZ (2006), *Konzept Flüchtlingspolitik im Rahmen der Entwicklungszusammenarbeit (BMZ aktuell No. 040)*, Bundesministerium für Wirtschaftliche Zusammenarbeit und Entwicklung, Bonn.

Born, H. (2009), "Security sector reform in challenging environments: Insights from a Comparative Analysis", in Born, H. and A. Schnabel (eds.), *Security sector reform in challenging environments*, DCAF, Geneva, http://www.gsdrc.org/document-library/security-sector-reform-in-challenging-environments-insights-from-comparative-analysis/.

Borton, J. (2004), *The Joint Evaluation of Emergency Assistance to Rwanda*, Humanitarian Practice Network, London, http://odihpn.org/magazine/the-joint-evaluation-of-emergency-assistance-to-rwanda/.

Brookings-Bern Project on Internal Displacement (2007), "Expert Seminar on Protracted IDP Situations", Brookings-Bern Project on Internal Displacement, Washington, DC, https://www.brookings.edu/wp-content/uploads/2012/04/20070621_displacement.pdf.

Caputo, E. et al. (2011), "Assessing the impacts of budget support: Case studies in Mali, Tunisia and Zambia", Evaluation Insights, No. 2, OECD Publishing, Paris, https://www.oecd.org/derec/50313762.pdf.

Carling, J. and C. Talleraas (2016), *Root Causes and Drivers of Migration: Implications for humanitarian efforts and development co-operation*, PRIO, Oslo.

CGD and IRC (2017), *Refugee Compacts: Addressing the Crisis of Protracted Displacement*, Center for Global Development, Washington, DC, https://www.cgdev.org/publication/refugee-compacts-addressing-the-crisis-of-protracted-displacement.

Chandran, R. et al. (2008), *Recovering from War: Gaps in Early Action*, DFID, London, https://www.alnap.org/system/files/content/resource/files/main/cic-e*arlyrecoveryfinal.pdf. CIC et al. (2015)*, Addressing Protracted Displacement: A Framework for Development-Humanitarian Cooperation, Center on International Cooperation, New York, http://cic.nyu.edu/sites/default/files/addressing_protracted_displacement_a_think_piece_dec_2015.pdf.

Cox, M. and K. Robson (2013), *Mid-Term Evaluation of the Budget Strengthening Initiative*, Agulhas, https://www.oecd.org/derec/unitedkingdom/Evaluation-Overseas-Development-Institute-Budget-Strengthening-Initiative.pdf.

Crawford, N. et al. (2015), *Protracted displacement: Uncertain paths to self-reliance in exile*, ODI, London, https://www.odi.org/publications/9906-refugee-idp-displacement-livelihoods-humanitarian-development.

Culbertson, S. et al. (2016), *Rethinking co-ordination of services to refugees in urban areas: Managing the crisis in Jordan and Lebanon*, RAND Corporation, Santa Monica, https://www.alnap.org/system/files/content/resource/files/main/rethinking-coordination-of-services-to-refugees.pdf.

Cummings, C. (15 March 2017), "Can Aid Stop Migration to Europe?", *Comment*, ODI, London, https://www.odi.org/comment/10496-can-aid-stop-migration-europe.

Dalrymple, S. and K. Smith (2015), *Coordinating Decision-Making: Meeting Needs – Mapping Donor Preferences in Humanitarian Response*, Development Initiatives, London, http://devinit.org/wp-content/uploads/2015/06/GHA-Inception-Report-Mapping-donor-funding-preferences.pdf.

Danida (2015), *Evaluation of the Strategy for Danish Humanitarian Action 2010-2015*, Ministry of Foreign Affairs of Denmark, Copenhagen, https://www.oecd.org/derec/denmark/Evaluation-strategy-Danish-humanitarian-action-2010-2015.pdf.

De Coning, C. and K. Friis (2011), "Coherence and Coordination: The Limits of the Comprehensive Approach", *Journal of International Peacekeeping*, Vol. 15, Brill, Leiden, pp. 243-272.

Derzsi-Horváth, A. et al. (2017), *Independent Grand Bargain Report*, GPPI, Berlin, http://www.gppi.net/publications/humanitarian-action/article/independent-grand-bargain-report/.

Development Initiatives (2017), *Global Humanitarian Assistance Report 2017*, Development Initiatives, New York, http://devinit.org/post/global-humanitarian-assistance-2017/.

Development Initiatives (2016), *Global Humanitarian Assistance Report 2016*, Development Initiatives, Bristol, http://devinit.org/post/global-humanitarian-assistance-report-2016/#.

Devictor, X. (2016), *Forcibly Displaced: Towards a Development Approach Supporting Refugees, the Internally Displaced, and their Hosts*, World Bank, Washington, DC, http://www.worldbank.org/en/events/2016/09/15/report-launch-forcibly-displaced-toward-a-development-approach-supporting-refugees-the-internally-displaced-and-their-hosts.

Devictor, X. and Q.T. Do (2016), "How Many Years Have Refugees Been in Exile", *World Bank Policy Research Working Paper*, No. September/7810, World Bank, Washington, DC, http://documents.worldbank.org/curated/en/549261472764700982/How-many-years-have-refugees-been-in-exile.

DFID (2002), *Conducting Conflict Assessments: Guidance Notes*, Department for International Development, London, http://www.conflictrecovery.org/bin/dfid-conflictassessmentguidance.pdf.

Dolan, C. (2003), *Collapsing Masculinities and Weak States: A Case Study of Northern Uganda*, Zed Books, London.

El Jack, A. (2003), *Gender and Armed Conflict: Overview Report*, BRIDGE, Institute of Development Studies, Brighton, http://www.bridge.ids.ac.uk/sites/bridge.ids.ac.uk/files/reports/CEP-Conflict-Report.pdf.

Evalnet (2010), *Development Evaluation Resources and Systems: A study of members of the OECD Network on Development Evaluation*, OECD Publishing, Paris.

Eyben, R. (2005), "Donors' Learning Difficulties: Results, Relationships and Responsibilities", *IDS Bulletin*, Vol. 36/3, Institute of Development Studies, Brighton, pp. 98-107.

Fabre, C. (2017a), "Localising the Response", *The Commitments Into Action Series*, OECD Publishing, Paris, https://www.oecd.org/development/humanitarian-donors/docs/Localisingtheresponse.pdf.

Fabre, C. (2017b), "Multi-year Humanitarian Funding", *The Commitments Into Action Series*, OECD Publishing, OECD, http://www.oecd.org/development/humanitarian-donors/docs/multiyearfunding.pdf.

Faguet, J. P. et al. (2014), "Does decentralization strengthen or weaken the state? Authority and social learning in a supple state", *Working Paper*, Department of International Development, London School of Economics and Political Science, London, http://eprints.lse.ac.uk/60631/1/Faguet_Fox_Poeschl_Does-decentralization-strengthen-or-weaken-the-state_WP_2014.pdf.

Faye, M. and P. Niehaus (2012), "Political aid cycles", *The American Economic Review*, Vol. 102/7, American Economic Association, Nashville, pp. 3516–3530.

Forced Displacement and Development Study Group (2017), "Refugee Compacts: Addressing the Crisis of Protracted Displacement", *CGD-IRC Brief*, CGD-IRC, Washington, DC, https://www.cgdev.org/publication/refugee-compacts-addressing-the-crisis-of-protracted-displacement.

Fratzke, S. (21 March 2016), "Move past the challenges and pitfalls in development-led responses to displacement", Devex, https://www.devex.com/news/move-past-the-challenges-and-pitfalls-in-development-led-responses-to-displacement-87898.

Glennie, J. and G. Rabinowitz (2013), *Localising Aid: a whole of society approach*, ODI, London, https://www.odi.org/publications/7571-localising-aid-whole-society-approach.

GSMA (2014), *Disaster Response: Mobile Money for the Displaced*, GSMA, London, https://www.gsma.com/mobilefordevelopment/wp-content/uploads/2015/01/Disaster-Response-Mobile-Money-for-the-Displaced.pdf.

Guterres, A. (18 January 2015), "Think the aid system can cope? It can't.", *World Economic Forum*, https://www.weforum.org/agenda/2015/01/think-the-aid-system-can-cope-it-cant/.

Hammond L. and I.D. Ali (2011), *Cash and Compassion: The Role of the Somali Diaspora in Relief, Development and Peace-building: Report of a Study Commissioned by UNDP Somalia*, United Nations Development Programme, New York, http://ussfs.org/sfs/wp-content/uploads/2012/07/somalidiaspora.pdf.

Harild, N. (2016), "Forced displacement: A development issue with humanitarian events", *Forced Migration Review*, Vol. 52, Refugee Studies Centre, Oxford, pp. 4-7.

High-Level Panel on Humanitarian Financing (2016), *Too important to fail – addressing the humanitarian financing gap*, OCHA, New York, https://reliefweb.int/sites/reliefweb.int/files/resources/%5BHLP%20Report%5D%20Too%20important%20to%20fail%E2%80%94addressing%20the%20humanitarian%20financing%20gap.pdf.

Hong, A. and A. Knoll (2016), *Strengthening the Migration-Development Nexus through Improved Policy and Institutional Coherence*, KNOMAD, Washington, DC.

House of Commons/International Development Committee (2017), *DFID's Use of Private Contractors*, House of Commons, London, https://publications.parliament.uk/pa/cm201617/cmselect/cmintdev/920/92002.htm.

Humanitarian Outcomes (2016), *Aid Worker Security Report 2016: Figures at a glance*, Humanitarian Outcomes, https://reliefweb.int/report/world/aid-worker-security-report-2016-figures-glance.

ICAI (2014), *How DFID Learns*, Independent Commission for Aid Impact, London, https://icai.independent.gov.uk/report/dfid-learns/.

IDMC (2017), *Global Report on Internal Displacement*, Internal Displacement Monitoring Centre, Oslo, http://www.internal-displacement.org/global-report/grid2017/.

IDMC (2016), *Global Report on Internal Displacement*, International Displacement Monitoring Centre, Oslo, http://www.internal-displacement.org/assets/publications/2016/2016-global-report-internal-displacement-IDMC.pdf.

IEG (2016), *World Bank Group Engagement in Situations of Fragility, Conflict and Violence*, Independent Evaluation Group, World Bank, Washington, DC, https://openknowledge.worldbank.org/handle/10986/24915.

IMF (2014), "Jordan", *IMF Country Report*, No. 14/153, International Monetary Fund, Washington, DC, https://www.imf.org/external/pubs/ft/scr/2014/cr14153.pdf.

IMF (2003), "External Debt Statistics: Guide for Compilers and Users", International Monetary Fund, https://www.imf.org/external/pubs/ft/eds/Eng/Guide/index.htm.

Irvine, J. (2016), *Global Civil Society Consultation on Migration and Local Development: A Synthesis Report in the context of the 3rd Global Mayoral Forum on Human Mobility*, JMDI, Brussels, http://migration4development.org/sites/default/files/report_cso_final-2.pdf.

ISSAT (2015), *What Works in International Security and Justice Programming?*, International Security Sector Advisory Team, DCAF, Geneva, http://issat.dcaf.ch/Learn/Resource-Library/Policy-and-Research-Papers/What-Works-in-International-Security-and-Justice-Programming.

Jacobsen, K. (1997),"Refugees' environmental impact: the effects of patterns of settlement", *Journal of Refugee Studies*, Vol. 10/1, Refugee Studies Centre, Oxford, pp. 19-36.

Jansury, L. et al. (2015), *Findings in Monitoring and Evaluation Practices in Humanitarian Emergencies*, George Washington University, Washington, DC, https://elliott.gwu.edu/sites/elliott.gwu.edu/files/IBTCI.pdf.

Jones, A. (2003), *Straight as a Rule: Heteronormativity, Gendercide, and the Non-Combatant Male*, Centro de Investigación y Docencia Económicas, Mexico City.

Kälin, W. and H.E. Chapuisat (2017), *Breaking the Impasse: Reducing protracted internal displacement as a collective outcome*, OCHA, New York, http://interactive.unocha.org/publication/2017_breaking_the_impasse/.

Knox, P.C. and J. Darcy (2014), *Insufficient evidence? The quality and use of evidence in humanitarian action*, ALNAP/ODI, London, https://www.alnap.org/system/files/content/resource/files/main/alnap-study-evidence.pdf.

Krystalli, R. and E. Ott (2015), *Evidence Synthesis in the Humanitarian Sector: A Humanitarian Evidence Programme Guidance Note*, Oxfam-Feinstein International Center, Somerville, http://fic.tufts.edu/assets/Humanitarian-Evidence-Program-Guidance-Note.pdf.

Kugiel, P. (14 December 2016),"Can Development Assistance Solve the Refugee Crisis?", *Polish Institute of International Affairs*, https://www.pism.pl/files/?id_plik=22655.

Kuhlman, T. (1991), "The economic integration of refugees in developing countries: A research model", *Journal of Refugee Studies*, Vol. 4/1, Refugee Studies Centre, Oxford, pp. 1-20.

Landry, J. (2013), "Displaced populations and their effects on regional stability", *Forced Migration Review*, Vol. 43, Refugee Studies Centre, Oxford, pp. 10-11.

Lawson, M.L. (2013), *Foreign Aid: International Donor Coordination of Development Assistance*, Congressional Research Service, Washington, DC, https://fas.org/sgp/crs/row/R41185.pdf.

Loescher, G. (1993), *Beyond Charity: International Co-operation and the Global Refugee Crisis*, Oxford University Press, New York.

Loescher, G. et al. (2008), *Protracted Refugee Situations: Political, Human Rights and Security Implications*, United Nations University, New York.

MacLeman, H. et al. (2016), *Resilience Systems Analysis: Learning & recommendations report*, OECD Publishing, Paris, https://www.oecd.org/dac/conflict-fragility-resilience/docs/SwedenLearning_Recommendationsreport.pdf.

Mallett, R. (2017), "Journeys on hold: How policy influences the migration decisions of Eritreans in Ethiopia", *Working Paper*, No. 506, ODI, London, https://www.odi.org/sites/odi.org.uk/files/resource-documents/11336.pdf.

Mathieu, A. (2017), *'We're here for an indefinite period'. Prospects for local integration of internally displaced people in North Kivu*, DRC, Oxfam International, Oxford, https://www.oxfam.org/en/research/were-here-indefinite-period-prospects-local-integration-internally-displaced-people-north.

McKechnie, A. and F. Davies (2013), *Localising Aid: Is it Worth the Risk?*, ODI, London, https://www.odi.org/sites/odi.org.uk/files/odi-assets/publications-opinion-files/8456.pdf.

Metcalfe-Hough, V. et al. (2017), *How to engage in long-term humanitarian crises: A desk review*, NORAD, Oslo, https://www.norad.no/globalassets/publikasjoner/publikasjoner-2017/evaluering/2.17-how-to-engage-in-long-term-humanitarian-crises_desk-review.pdf.

MICIC (2016), *Guidelines to protect migrants in countries experiencing conflict or natural disaster*, Migrants in Countries in Crisis Initiative, Geneva, https://micicinitiative.iom.int/sites/default/files/document/micic_guidelines_english_web_13_09_2016.pdf.

Miller, S. D. and J. Lehmann (2016), *The Challenges of Building Capacities for Refugee Protection*, GPPi, Berlin, http://www.gppi.net/publications/human-rights/article/the-challenges-of-building-capacities-for-refugee-protection/.

Milner, J. (2016), "When Norms are Not Enough: Understanding the Principle and Practice of Burden and Responsibility Sharing for Refugees", *Global Leadership and Cooperation for Refugees Series*, Paper no. 2, CIGI, Waterloo, https://www.cigionline.org/sites/default/files/documents/Refugee%20Paper%20no2web_3.pdf.

Moore, W. H. and S. Shellman (2007), "Whither will they go? A global analysis of refugee flows, 1955-1995", *International Studies Quarterly*, Vol. 51, Wiley, Hoboken, pp. 811-834.

Morrison-Métois, S. (2017), *Responding to Refugee Crises in Developing Countries: What Can We Learn from Evaluations? South Sudan Case Study*, OECD Publishing, Paris.

Mosel, I. and S. Levine (2014), *Remaking the case for linking relief, rehabilitation, and development: How LRRD can become a practically useful concept for assistance in difficult places*, Humanitarian Policy Group at the Overseas Development Institute, London, https://www.odi.org/sites/odi.org.uk/files/odi-assets/publications-opinion-files/8882.pdf.

Mowjee, T. et al. (2015), *Coherence in Conflict: Bringing humanitarian and development aid streams together*, Danida, Copenhagen, https://www.humanitarianoutcomes.org/file/77/download?token=P99VgU7j.

Norad (2015), *Striking the Balance: Evaluation of the Planning, Organisation and Management of Norwegian Assistance Related to the Syrian Regional Crisis*, Norwegian Agency for Development Cooperation, Oslo.

O'Dwyer, B. (2005), "Stakeholder democracy: challenges and contributions from social accounting", *Business Ethics: A European Review*, Vol 14/1, Wiley, Hoboken, pp. 28-41.

Obrecht, A. et al. (2017), "Evaluation humanitarian innovation", *HIF-ALNAP Working Paper*, ODI/ALNAP, London, https://www.alnap.org/help-library/evaluating-humanitarian-innovation-hif-alnap-working-paper.

OCHA (2017), *Global Humanitarian Overview 2017*, UN Office for the Coordination of Humanitarian Affairs, New York, https://www.unocha.org/sites/unocha/files/GHO_2017.pdf.

OCHA (2015), *The 2015 UN Coordinated Appeals: An ambitious plan to meet growing humanitarian needs*, UN Office for the Coordination of Humanitarian Affairs, New York, http://devinit.org/wp-content/uploads/2015/04/The-2015-UN-coordinated-appeals-F.pdf.

OECD (2017a), *Development aid rises again in 2016*, OECD Publishing, Paris, https://www.oecd.org/dac/financing-sustainable-development/development-finance-data/ODA-2016-detailed-summary.pdf.

OECD (2017b), *Development Co-operation Report 2017: Data for Development*, OECD Publishing, Paris. http://dx.doi.org/10.1787/dcr-2017-en

OECD (2016a), "Are there alternative pathways for refugees?", *Migration Policy Debates*, No. 12, OECD Publishing, Paris, https://www.oecd.org/els/mig/migration-policy-debates-12.pdf.

OECD (2016b), *Development Co-operation Report 2016: The Sustainable Development Goals as Business Opportunities*, OECD Publishing, Paris, http://dx.doi.org/10.1787/dcr-2016-en.

OECD (2016c), *Evaluation Systems in Development Cooperation: 2016 Review*, OECD Publishing, Paris, http://dx.doi.org/10.1787/9789264262065-en.

OECD (2016d), *Good development support in fragile, at-risk and crisis affected contexts*, OECD Publishing, Paris, http://dx.doi.org/10.1787/24140929.

OECD (2016e), *States of Fragility 2016: Understanding Violence*, OECD Publishing, Paris, http://dx.doi.org/10.1787/9789264267213-en.

OECD (2015), *Development Assistance and Approaches to Risk in Fragile and Conflict Affected States*, OECD Publishing, Paris.

OECD (2014a), *Development Co-operation Report 2014: Mobilising Resources for Sustainable Development*, OECD Publishing, Paris, http://dx.doi.org/10.1787/20747721.

OECD (2014b), *Guidelines for resilience systems analysis*, OECD Publishing, Paris, https://www.oecd.org/dac/Resilience%20Systems%20Analysis%20FINAL.pdf.

OECD (2011a), *International Engagement in Fragile States: Can't we do better?*, OECD Publishing, Paris, http://dx.doi.org/10.1787/9789264086128-en.

OECD (2011b), *Managing Aid Seminar: Using evidence to improve aid policies and demonstrate results*, OECD Publishing, Paris.

OECD (2008), "Whole-of-Government Approaches to Fragile States", *OECD Journal on Development*, Vol. 8/3. http://dx.doi.org/10.1787/journal_dev-v8-art39-en

OECD (2005/2008), *The Paris Declaration on Aid Effectiveness and the Accra Agenda for Action*, OECD Publishing, Paris, https://www.oecd.org/dac/effectiveness/34428351.pdf.

OECD (2005), *The Paris Declaration on Aid Effectiveness*, OECD Publishing, Paris, http://dx.doi.org/10.1787/9789264098084-en.

OECD (2003), *Harmonising donor practices for effective aid delivery*, OECD Publishing, Paris, http://dx.doi.org/10.1787/19900988.

Otto, R. and L. Weingärtner (2013), *Linking Relief and Development: More than old solutions for old problems?*, Dutch Ministry of Foreign Affairs, The Hague, https://www.government.nl/binaries/government/documents/reports/2013/05/01/iob-study-linking-relief-and-development-more-than-old-solutions-for-old-problems/iob-study-linking-relief-and-development-more-than-old-solutions-for-old-problems.pdf.

Pavanello, S. (24 November 2008), "What does 'early recovery' mean?", *Comment*, ODI, https://www.odi.org/comment/2551-does-early-recovery-mean.

Poole, L. (2014), *A Calculated Risk: How Donors Should Engage with Risk Financing and Transfer Mechanisms*, OECD Publishing, Paris, https://www.oecd.org/dac/A%20calculated%20risk.pdf.

PRMN (2017), *Somalia: Displacements dashboard*, Protection & Return Monitoring Network, UNHCR, Geneva, https://data2.unhcr.org/en/documents/details/58901.

Puri, J. et al. (2014), "What methods may be used in impact evaluations of humanitarian assistance", *Working Paper*, No. 22, International Initiative for Impact Evaluation, New Delhi, https://www.alnap.org/system/files/content/resource/files/main/wp-22-humanitarian-methods-working-paper-top.pdf.

Rabinowitz, G. (4 July 2013), "Localising aid to NGOs: issues and challenges highlighted by a multi-country study", *Comment*, ODI, London, https://www.odi.org/comment/7578-local-capacity-localising-aid-ngos-donors-hiv-aids.

Rao, M. P. et al. (2014), *Final external evaluation of Somali institutional development project*, UNDP, New York, https://erc.undp.org/evaluation/evaluations/detail/6147.

Richmond, A. H. (1993), "Reactive Migration: Sociological Perspectives on Refugee Movements", *Journal of Refugee Studies*, Refugee Studies Centre, Oxford, Vol. 6, pp. 7-24.

Rother, B. et al. (2016), *The Economic Impact of Conflicts and the Refugee Crisis in the Middle East and North Africa*, IMF, Washington, DC, https://www.imf.org/en/Publications/Staff-Discussion-Notes/Issues/2016/12/31/The-Economic-Impact-of-Conflicts-and-the-Refugee-Crisis-in-the-Middle-East-and-North-Africa-44228.

Ruaudel, H. and S. Morrison-Métois (2017), "Responding to Refugee Crises in Developing Countries: What Can We Learn From Evaluations?", *OECD Development Co-operation Working Papers*, No. 37, OECD Publishing, Paris, http://dx.doi.org/10.1787/ae4362bd-en.

Scott, J. M. and C.A. Steele (2011), "Sponsoring democracy: the United States and democracy aid to the developing world, 1988–2001", *International Studies Quarterly*, Vol 55/1, Wiley, Hoboken, pp. 47-69.

Scott, R. (2015), *Financing in Crisis? Making humanitarian finance fit for the future*, OECD Publishing, Paris, http://www.oecd.org/dac/OECD-WP-Humanitarian-Financing-Crisis%20.pdf.

SDC (2016), *Discussion Note: Forced Displacement and Development*, Swiss Agency for Development and Cooperation, Bern, http://mdgglobalmeeting2016.org/wp-content/uploads/2016/05/Global-Meeting-2016-Forced-Displacement-and-Development-Discussion-Note-.pdf.

SDSN (2015), *Investment Needs to Achieve the Sustainable Development Goals: Understanding the Billions and Trillions*, UN Sustainable Development Solutions Network, New York, http://unsdsn.org/resources/publications/sdg-investment-needs/.

Shellman, S. M. and B.M. Stewart (2007), "Predicting risk factors associated with forced migration: An early warning model of Haitian flight", *Civil Wars*, Vol 9/2, Taylor and Francis, Abingdon, pp. 174-199.

Sida (2016), *Designing relief and development to enhance resilience and impact*, Swedish International Development Cooperation Agency, Stockholm.

SIGAR (2015), *Afghan Refugees and Returnees: Corruption and Lack of Afghan Ministerial Capacity Have Prevented Implementation of a Long-term Refugee Strategy*, Special Inspector General for Afghan Reconstruction, Arlington, https://www.sigar.mil/pdf/audits/SIGAR-15-83-AR.pdf.

Sjostedt, M. (2013), "Aid effectiveness and the Paris Declaration: a mismatch between ownership and results-based management", *Public Administration and Development*, Vol. 33, Wiley, Hoboken, pp. 143-155.

Sjostedt, M. and A. Sundstrom (2017), "Donor co-ordination or donor confusion? How disputed problem framing affects the prospects for aid harmonization", *Development Policy Review*, Vol. 35/S2, Overseas Development Institute, London, pp. 064-069.

Stamnes, E. (2016), *Rethinking the Humanitarian-Development Nexus*, Norwegian Institute of International Affairs, Oslo, https://brage.bibsys.no/xmlui/bitstream/handle/11250/2405657/NUPI%2bPolicy%2bBrief-24-16-Eli%2bStamnes-2.pdf?sequence=3&isAllowed=y.

Steets, J. et al. (2011). *Donor Strategies for Addressing the Transition Gap and Linking Humanitarian and Development Assistance*, Global Public Policy Institute, Berlin, http://www.gppi.net/fileadmin/user_upload/media/pub/2011/steets_2011_transition_web.pdf.

Steiner, N. et al. (2003), *Problems of Protection: The UNHCR, Refugees, and Human Rights*, Routledge, London.

Stuart, E. et al. (2016), *Leaving no one behind: A critical path for the first 1,000 days of the Sustainable Development Goals*, ODI, London, https://www.odi.org/sites/odi.org.uk/files/resource-documents/10691.pdf.

Taylor, G. et al. (2015), *Review of the Netherlands Humanitarian Assistance 2009-2014*, Netherlands Ministry of Foreign Affairs, The Hague, https://www.humanitarianoutcomes.org/file/67/download?token=mMdzD22n.

Taylor, J. E. (2016) "Economic Impact of Refugees", *Proceedings of the National Academy of Sciences of the United States of America*, Vol. 113/27, National Academy of Sciences, Washington, DC, pp. 7449-7453.

Thomas, M. (2017), *"Understanding Humanitarian Funds: Going beyond Country-based Pooled Funds"*, NRC, Oslo, https://www.nrc.no/globalassets/pdf/reports/pooled_funds_2017_16mar2017_web_v2.pdf.

Thomson, J. (2017), "The Role of Resettlement in Refugee Responsibility Sharing", *Global Leadership and Cooperation for Refugees Series*, Paper no. 3, CIGI, Waterloo, https://www.cigionline.org/sites/default/files/documents/Refugee%20Paper%20no.3_0.pdf.

Turk, V. (2016), "Prospects for Responsibility Sharing in a Refugee Context", *Journal on Migration and Human Security*, Vol. 4/3, Center for Migration Studies, New York, pp. 45-59.

UN Global Pulse (2017), *Integrating Big Data into the Monitoring and Evaluation of Development Programmes*, UN Global Pulse, New York, https://www.unglobalpulse.org/big-data-monitoring-and-evaluation-report.

UNDP (2016a), "Advancing Development Approaches to Migration and Displacement", *Position Paper for the 2016 UN Summit for Refugees and Migrants*, UNDP, New York, http://www.undp.org/content/undp/en/home/librarypage/poverty-reduction/position-paper-for-the-2016-un-summit-for-refugees-and-migrants-.html.

UNDP (201bc), *Guidance Note: A Development Approach to Migration and Displacement*, United Nations Development Programme, New York, http://www.undp.org/content/undp/en/home/librarypage/poverty-reduction/guidance-note---migration-and-displacement.html.

UNDP (2016c), *Promoting Development Approaches to Migration and Displacement: Five UNDP Specific Focus Areas*, United Nations Development Programme, New York, http://www.undp.org/content/dam/undp/library/Sustainable%20Development/Migration%20 and%20displacement/UNDP%20Booklet%205%20Things_low_V6.pdf?download.

UNDP (2016d), *The State of Resilience Programming – The Syria Regional Refugee and Resilience Plan (3RP)*, UNDP, Amman, www.arabstates.undp.org/.../SyriaResponse/UNDP_Resilience-3RP_final-lowres.pdf

UNDP (2013), *Resilience-Based Development Responses to the Syria Crisis*, United Nations Development Programme, New York, http://www.undp.org/content/dam/undp/library/crisis%20prevention/UNDP_SYR_brochurev2_20140901.pdf.

UNDP et al. (2016), *Durable Solutions: Preliminary Operational Guide*, United Nations Development Programme, New York, https://reliefweb.int/sites/reliefweb.int/files/resources/durable_solutions_guide_011116.pdf.

UNHCR (2017), *Global Trends Report 2016*, UN Refugee Agency, Geneva, http://www.unhcr.org/5943e8a34.pdf.

UNHCR (2016a), *2016 Jordan Refugee Response: Protection Sector Operational Strategy*, Protection Working Group, UN Refugee Agency, Geneva, https://data2.unhcr.org/en/documents/download/43783.

UNHCR (2016b), *Global Trends: Forced Displacement in 2015*, UN Refugee Agency, Geneva, http://www.unhcr.org/en-us/statistics/unhcrstats/576408cd7/unhcr-global-trends-2015.html.

UNHCR (2016c), *Mid-Year Trends 2016*, UN Refugee Agency, Geneva, http://www.unhcr.org/en-us/statistics/unhcrstats/58aa8f247/mid-year-trends-june-2016.html.

UNHCR (2014), *UNHCR Statistical Yearbook 2014*, UN Refugee Agency, Geneva, http://www.unhcr.org/en-us/statistics/country/566584fc9/unhcr-statistical-yearbook-2014-14th-edition.html.

UNHCR (2005), *Handbook for Planning and Implementing: Development Assistance for Refugees (DAR) Programmes*, UN Refugee Agency, Geneva, http://www.unhcr.org/publications/operations/44c4875c2/handbook-planning-implementing-development-assistance-refugees-dar-programmes.html.

UNHCR Excom (2017), *Resilience and self-reliance from a protection and solutions perspective*, UN Refugee Agency, Geneva, http://www.unhcr.org/en-us/excom/standcom/58ca4f827/resilience-self-reliance-protection-solutions-perspective.html.

UNHCR Excom (2016), *Livelihoods and self-reliance*, UN Refugee Agency, Geneva, http://www.unhcr.org/576ba7257.pdf.

UNHCR ExCom (2009), *Conclusion on Protracted Refugee Situations*, UNHCR, Geneva, http://www.unhcr.org/en-us/excom/exconc/4b332bca9/conclusion-protracted-refugee-situations.html.

UNHCR Excom (1997), EC/47/SC/CRP.7: *Social and economic impact of large refugee populations on host developing countries*, UN Refugee Agency, Geneva, http://www.unhcr.org/en-us/excom/standcom/3ae68d0e10/social-economic-impact-large-refugee-populations-host-developing-countries.html.

Van-Hear, N. (2003), "Refugee Diasporas, Remittances, Development, and Conflict", MPI, https://www.migrationpolicy.org/article/refugee-diasporas-remittances-development-and-conflict.

Van Veen, E. and V. Dudouet (2017), *Hitting the target but missing the point: Assessing donor support for inclusive and legitimate politics in fragile states*, OECD, Paris, https://www.oecd.org/dac/conflict-fragility-resilience/docs/Hitting_the_target.pdf.

Vemuru, V. et al. (2016), *Refugee Impacts on Turkana Hosts: A Social Impact Analysis for Kakuma Town and Refugee Camp, Turkana County, Kenya*, World Bank, Washington, DC, http://documents.worldbank.org/curated/en/359161482490953624/Refugee-impacts-on-Turkana-hosts-a-social-impact-analysis-for-Kakuma-town-and-refugee-camp-Turkana-County-Kenya.

Vowles, P. (4 September 2016), "Finding Failure", Medium, https://medium.com/@PeteVowles/finding-failure-d0b365cc649d.

WEF (2016), *Global Risks Report 2016*, World Economic Forum, Geneva, https://www.weforum.org/reports/the-global-risks-report-2016.

Whitfield, L. (2009), *The politics of aid: African strategies for dealing with donors*, Oxford University Press, Oxford.

World Bank (2017), *Forcibly Displaced: Towards a Development Approach to Supporting Refugees, the Internally Displaced and their Hosts*, World Bank, Washington, DC, http://www.worldbank.org/en/events/2016/09/15/report-launch-forcibly-displaced-toward-a-development-approach-supporting-refugees-the-internally-displaced-and-their-hosts.

World Bank Development Committee (2016), *Forced Displacement and Development*, World Bank, Washington, DC, http://siteresources.worldbank.org/DEVCOMMINT/Documentation/23713856/DC2016-0002-FDD.pdf.

World Bank Group (2016), *Municipalities at the forefront of the Syrian refugee crisis*, World Bank, Washington, DC, http://www.worldbank.org/en/news/feature/2016/08/03/municipalities-at-the-forefront-of-the-syrian-refugee-crisis.

World Humanitarian Summit (2016), "World Humanitarian Summit Documents: Core Commitments", World Humanitarian Summit, http://www.agendaforhumanity.org/resources/world-humanitarian-summit#core-commitments.

Zetter, R. (2015), *Protection in Crisis: Forced Migration and Protection in a Global Era*, Migration Policy Institute, Washington, DC, https://www.migrationpolicy.org/research/protection-crisis-forced-migration-and-protection-global-era.

Zetter, R. (2012), *Guidelines for Assessing the Impacts and Costs of Forced Displacement*, World Bank, Washington, DC, http://siteresources.worldbank.org/EXTSOCIALDEVELOPMENT/Resources/244362-1265299949041/6766328-1265299960363/SME338-Impac-Report_v8.pdf.

Zyck, S. and H. Krebs (2015), *Localising humanitarianism: improving effectiveness through inclusive action*, Humanitarian Policy Group, London.

Addressing Forced Displacement through Development Planning and Co-operation: Guidance for Donor Policy Makers and Practitioners

The Organisation for Economic Co-operation and Development (OECD) Development Assistance Committee (DAC) is the leading international forum for bilateral providers of development co-operation. Its main objective is to promote development co-operation and other policies so as to contribute to sustainable development. The Committee monitors development finance flows, reviews and provides guidance on development co-operation policies, promotes sharing of good practices, and helps shape the global development architecture.

The DAC currently has 30 members. Since its establishment, the DAC has taken key decisions on and set standards for development co-operation. The DAC defines official development assistance (ODA) and periodically updates the list of ODA recipients. It sets standards on the financial terms and conditions of aid and has agreed to untie most development co-operation to the least developed and heavily indebted poor countries.

The DAC also helps shape the international development agenda by developing policy guidance in many areas, including gender equality, harmonisation of donor practices and policy coherence for development assistance. As a standard setter and watchdog of development co-operation, the DAC remains relevant not only for its members, but also to the development community more generally.

In February 2016, the members of the DAC convened a high-level meeting. At this meeting, DAC members noted that the world was experiencing multiple large-scale refugee movements that were applying pressure in countries of origin, transit and destination. They recognised the need for comprehensive and co-ordinated international responses. They also emphasised that in situations of protracted crises, co-operation providers needed to develop models for better co-ordination and planning between development humanitarian actors and host countries to make official development assistance (ODA) more effective.

The DAC Temporary Working Group (TWG) on Refugees and Migration was subsequently established with a one-year mandate to respond to the needs identified at the 2016 high-level meeting. The TWG has developed this guidance for donor staff in headquarters and field offices seeking to improve development planning and co-operation in situations of forced displacement. The guidance will also help other key stakeholders better understand donor priorities and responses in situations of forced displacement, while enabling delivery partners to work alongside donors with greater insight and improved efficiency.

 www.oecd.org/dac

@OECDdev
www.twitter.com/OECDdev

THE DEVELOPMENT ASSISTANCE COMMITTEE:
ENABLING EFFECTIVE DEVELOPMENT

ORGANISATION FOR ECONOMIC CO-OPERATION AND DEVELOPMENT

The OECD is a unique forum where governments work together to address the economic, social and environmental challenges of globalisation. The OECD is also at the forefront of efforts to understand and to help governments respond to new developments and concerns, such as corporate governance, the information economy and the challenges of an ageing population. The Organisation provides a setting where governments can compare policy experiences, seek answers to common problems, identify good practice and work to co-ordinate domestic and international policies.

The OECD member countries are: Australia, Austria, Belgium, Canada, Chile, the Czech Republic, Denmark, Estonia, Finland, France, Germany, Greece, Hungary, Iceland, Ireland, Israel, Italy, Japan, Korea, Latvia, Luxembourg, Mexico, the Netherlands, New Zealand, Norway, Poland, Portugal, the Slovak Republic, Slovenia, Spain, Sweden, Switzerland, Turkey, the United Kingdom and the United States. The European Union takes part in the work of the OECD.

OECD Publishing disseminates widely the results of the Organisation's statistics gathering and research on economic, social and environmental issues, as well as the conventions, guidelines and standards agreed by its members.

OECD PUBLISHING, 2, rue André-Pascal, 75775 PARIS CEDEX 16
(43 2017 09 1 P) ISBN 978-92-64-28558-3 – 2017